PRAISE FOR *NC*

MW01291367

Rarely have I read a book to endorse, which impacted me as much as this one. As I looked through the pages, it shone a light into the recesses of my own heart. Rebecca tells us that the abundant life is not a healthy bank balance, but it is remembering what the Lord has done for us and where we came from. It is a vital read to illuminate our lives and bring us to a place where Christ is central.

This book is from a genuine heart which has learned to turn tragedy into triumph and brings us back into the real world where Christ would want us to be. If anyone is depressed, sad, lonely, has relationship problems or is under pressure, or conversely, if they believe they are in a good place, then this book is an essential read.

—COLIN J. COOPER, Founder of Cathedral House, Chairman of Ministers Fellowship Global (Huddersfield, ENGLAND)

A couple of centuries ago, a young pastor named Henry Scougal wrote a small book entitled *The Life of God in the Soul of Man*. As I read Rebecca's book, *No Ordinary Days*, all I could think about was the life of God in the soul of Rebecca Jacob. This is one of the most transparent books that I have ever read. Rebecca hides nothing of the real disappointments and struggles that she has had over the years in her walk with the Lord. She shares honestly and yet with an amazing down to earth sense of humor. If in your life you have been ambushed, crushed, or thrown off track, and you are wondering if there is any hope at all, you need to read her book!

—ROBERTO EVANS, pastor, international conference speaker, author of *El Ayudador* (Morelia, MEXICO)

I am so excited to share this story with people who are walking this same path. It is an inspiring, practical guide, filled with wit and humor. I've seen Rebecca walk this out in the hardest of days. Even in her pain, she found the time and strength to walk with us through some of our darkest days. This book is an excellent "tool box" of how she did it, and still does it!

—JANA LACKEY, Co-founder of Love Botswana Ministries, www.lovebotswana.org (Maun, BOTSWANA)

I must confess that before I finished the first paragraph, I knew that *No Ordinary Days* would be a very good book. But as I read on, page after page, my next thought was: this book is so good, so deep, so real, so honest, Rebecca should have been writing many books her entire Christian life!

Rebecca has the gift of effortlessly and flawlessly blending the practical and the profound with home-spun and scholarly tones that flow together with such beauty and undeniable clarity, that again and again I found myself saying, "Of course, why didn't I see that before?" But let me warn you, I would not recommend this book to anyone who is afraid of 'self-discovery'. Her honesty is contagious. Beyond the depth of Christian truth, thought, and feeling, the simplicity of Rebecca's prose and poetic imagination at times soars.

—ELLIOTT TEPPER, Founder and CEO of Betel Internacional, poet, author of *At the Turning of the Tides* (Madrid, SPAIN)

With transparency and humor, my friend Rebecca has written a wonderful memoir of her experiences in the fiery furnace of rejection and pain. Yet she has come through it "without the smell of smoke" on her (Daniel 3:27). While owning up to the human frailties all of us grapple with, she reminds us that when we seek His help, Jesus always is there to offer acceptance, hope, and direction for the future. You will be edified and blessed as you journey with her through *No Ordinary Days*.

—RUTHANNE GARLOCK, coauthor of *A Woman's Guide to Spiritual Warfare* and *Praying Prodigals Home* (San Antonio, UNITED STATES)

No Ordinary Days

No Ordinary Days

Growth Happens in Unexpected Places

REBECCA M. JACOB

XULON PRESS

Xulon Press
2301 Lucien Way #415
Maitland, FL 32751
407.339.4217
www.xulonpress.com

COVER DESIGN BY AHMED MANRIQUEZ; www.holacocored.com
Instagram@amanriq/Linkedin:amanriq

PHOTOGRAPHY BY THE BIALONS VIA UNSPLASH;
Instagram.com/the.bialons

PORTRAIT PHOTOGRAPHER BY NEPTUNO JORDACHE

Unless otherwise indicated, Scripture quotations taken from the Holy Bible,
New International Version (NIV). Copyright © 1973, 1978, 1984, 2011 by Biblica,
Inc.™. Used by permission. All rights reserved.

Paperback ISBN-13: 978-1-6628-2044-1
eBook ISBN-13: 978-1-6628-2045-8

To my kids, Ryan and Jaz, who face their days with grace and courage.

Table of Contents

Foreword

met Rebecca in 1979, when we were both brides. Drawn to her sharp sense of humor and passion for adventure while serving Jesus, I hoped we would become friends. For 40 years, we have shared the journey of ministry and friendship. We have walked and talked and dined (from picnic to banquet) in many nations. Rebecca taught me cafe etiquette in Madrid and how to tell if the *tortilla de patata* was homemade. We tasted Peking duck in Beijing and fried goat in Myanmar. Rebecca loves the nations, their inhabitants, and their food.

While planning the first of our daughters' weddings (we are blessed with three lovely daughters), I sent an invitation to Rebecca in Spain, mostly as a courtesy. I never dreamed she would make the investment in time and travel to attend. I recall her words as she gave her RSVP by phone call, "Of course I'm coming, Nancy. You're my friend, and this is what friends do!" Being foodies, we still occasionally daydream about the deliciousness of that particular wedding cake, a succulent white layer cake with passion fruit curd.

Jesus stood on the shore of Galilee and spoke this promise, "Blessed are those who hunger and thirst for righteousness, for they will be filled." Matthew 5:6. *The Message* version says, "You're blessed when you've worked up a good appetite for God. He's food and drink in the best meal you'll ever eat." Through her engaging style and honest perspective, Rebecca invites us to the table for food that truly satisfies, and the pure water freely offered to quench our deepest longings. As I read *No Ordinary Days*, I was beckoned to return to the simplicity of hungering and thirsting for God. May it be the same for you, dear reader.

Nancy Pennington, M.A.
Vice President, Firefall International

Introduction

Even though my marriage failed on the mission field in Spain, God lovingly led me and helped me face every stage of life with humor and grace. This isn't an autobiographical book of wild and wooly tales, but about everyday life, looked at from a fresh vantage point. *No Ordinary Days* isn't about learning valuable lessons but about opening our eyes to see God's goodness through unplanned encounters and experiences in everyday life.

If you think you might get preached at, you can relax. You won't. It's not meant to be a sermon or lecture and certainly doesn't give three easy steps to a fulfilling Christian experience or five to perfect behavior. I desire that the readers gain a greater understanding of God's workings by recognizing that things don't always turn out the way they prayed, and victory often looks different than hoped.

And that's OK. It's OK because God is present during head-on collisions with the unexpected, and He is accessible to clear the way when you see roadblocks up ahead. Rather than fixing outward and temporary circumstances, He is working something lasting in us that changes the way we approach life.

I'd like to invite you to travel along with me and see how an ordinary day can become extraordinary when we walk with our eyes open to the goodness of God and aware of the sweetness of life.

Acknowledgments

Once in a while a friend or acquaintance would say to me, "You should write a book" and my usual response was, "What can I say that hasn't been said and besides, I have no original thought; everything I know I learned from someone else." But as time went by, I began to wonder if maybe something I had to say could help someone. Along the way friends have encouraged me, and helped me hear the Holy Spirit whisper in agreement. Many people have been involved in this book, but several stand out to me.

I would have given up on this endeavor a long time ago had it not been for friends assuring me that I have stories to tell. The two I think of first are Arnold Pust and Josh Farrar; if two young men thought my words were worth reading, then maybe they were, so I kept typing. Thanks, guys.

I'm indebted to my sister Paula, and to Mary Lou and Lisa, "mis comadres para siempre", who made me stick to it; just the thought of us together makes me chuckle.

Thanks, Joyce Creed, for the first edits and friendship. There are no friends, like old friends.

Beverly Shay, thanks for being the grammar police; you deserve a badge.

Gwendolyn Rowland, you helped keep me real and honest. *"Mi sobrina, guapa y fina"*—you are one of a kind.

Nancy Pennington, thanks for being a friend. We might not always have Paris, but we will always have that public restroom in the train station in Bordeaux.

Paula Shields, thank you for your example of following Jesus to the ends of the earth to bind up wounds and heal broken hearts.

I owe much to my church and the elders. A few years ago, someone asked me who my spiritual heroes were; after just a minute's thought, I said, "The elders, because I know them, and they walk their talk." I'm grateful for their love, support, and encouragement during the darkest time of my life and ministry. Gracias Flores, Antonio, Jose Luis, Jose Carlos y Dorita.

My parents Wayne and Martha Myers, who are in their 90s now, have shown me what a life of passion looks like and that it is possible to live for Jesus every day and every decade. They get nicer, sweeter, and more generous with every passing year.

There are so many others that have spoken into my life, lifted me up, hung out, and laughed till we cried so many times, in so many places, that I will need another book just to tell about it. Friends, you know who you are.

CHAPTER 1

Blindsided

My husband left the week of our 25th wedding anniversary, and up until then, things, in general, had gone pretty well. People had often commented on how blessed my life was, and I wholeheartedly agreed. I had an abundance of the important things in life. I was healthy, had plenty, and felt close to family and friends. I had never experienced abandonment or abuse, and was aware that I was loved by God, by my parents, and by the people important to me.

The nagging hurt so familiar to many from early childhood was now new to me at middle age. For the first time, I felt the agony of not being wanted by someone I loved deeply and was helpless to do anything about it.

I knew what it was like to walk on solid ground, but now I was learning to tread water and trying not to drown in an ocean of new negative feelings and piercing pain. I began to wonder if something was physically wrong with me when I noticed pressure settling in my chest. Although not a crushing weight, it was always there, not piercing enough to send me to the

ER, but constant enough to concern me. I mentioned it to my friend Molly. "It's grief, Rebecca. Grief hurts."

During my years of ministry, I had listened to and prayed with many grieving people and met people with pain so deeply rooted in their lives that it affected not only their quality of life but also bled onto everyone around them. I had read about all the steps of grief, some said five, some seven, but all said some people never recover; they get stuck in one of the stages and live there forever. Their grief becomes lodged, and they become lifeless and sterile. I knew I didn't want to be one of those people, but I was also aware that I didn't have it in myself to "get over it."

Friends encouraged me, "You have to go on with your life." And I knew it was true, but I also knew I was not strong or resilient. Many people came through for me with phone calls and visits, shopping trips, and lunch outings. They gave what they had, and it was much appreciated, but the help I needed to make me whole had to be supernatural.

I knew I would have to avail myself of the resources of healing that Jesus had purchased on the Cross and so generously extended to me and to all who were hurting. He had not become a man, died, and raised back to life for me to live a powerless life, dragging around draped in sadness and gloom for the rest of my life.

The prophet Isaiah foretold Jesus' mission: "The Spirit of the Sovereign Lord is on me, because the Lord has anointed me to proclaim good news to the poor. He has sent me to bind up the broken-hearted, to proclaim freedom for the captives and release from darkness for the prisoners, to proclaim the year of the Lord's favor and the day of vengeance of our God, to comfort all who mourn, and provide for those who grieve in Zion—to bestow on them a crown of beauty instead of ashes, the oil of joy instead of mourning, and a garment of praise instead of a spirit of despair. They will be called oaks of righteousness, a planting of the Lord for the display of his splendor." (Isaiah 61:1-3)

He freely offered relief: beauty, joy, and praise so I could be planted and He would be glorified. And that was my desire; it had been my desire from the moment I gave my life to Him and then started in ministry. I wanted my roots to go deep in Jesus, so my Savior would receive glory from my life. I wanted all I was and all I did to point to Him. But it seemed harder now. How could this broken marriage and broken life ever end up giving Him glory? The whole situation seemed so wrong—the opposite of what I had worked for and expected from a life given in sacrifice to God and others.

But I wanted my life to bring Him praise, to make Him proud. So, I started doing what I could.

Every day, before I got up and put my feet on the floor, I said Psalm 188:24 out loud: *"This is the day that the Lord has made; I will rejoice and be glad in it."* Then I slipped on my robe and went downstairs to read the Word and pray. That declaration set the tone for the day. I had proclaimed the day I was about to live had been made by God, and I was going to celebrate that fact by being glad. Because He had gifted me with a new day, I could and would rejoice.

The future looked bleak and hard, but I had this one day, and I knew if I trusted Him, He would help me make it through the next few hours, doing what needed to be done. I would ask for help for *this* day He had made. I could receive His heavenly assistance to keep the house going, encourage my daughter, who was still at home, and serve the church. I could do at least *one* more day with His support. I went to Him for the daily help His generous heart extended.

How sad when people reject the hand He offers and run *from* Him instead of *to* Him, and rail at Him instead of leaning into Him. I've watched them rant and rave and shake their fists heavenward, demanding explanations, answers, and heavenly apologies they are never going to get. How much better it would be if they would just approach the throne of grace and whisper, "Help me." Isn't that what we need? We need help; help to go on, help to get better, help to swim out of the deep where we can't touch the bottom, and onto the shore of sanity and wholeness. We need help. We need *His* help.

I took His hand and asked Him for intervention, but that's not all I did. I also thanked Him. The rug had been pulled out from under me; I had been blindsided by the breakup of my marriage, and my future was uncertain. But even in sadness, I wasn't blind to the blessings surrounding me.

Oh my, so much to be thankful for! I would start by being thankful for a roof over my head. "Some women are left on the street," I reminded myself and rejoiced in my comfortable surroundings. I thanked Him for my eyes and my ears. How much more challenging it would be to face an uncertain future, blind or deaf! At least, I could hear; at least, I could see. "Thank you. Thank you, Jesus."

It may sound silly, but that daily morning exercise protected me from self-pity. When faced with the unfairness of life, feeling sorry for ourselves is tempting; it appears to be comforting, but ultimately, it's a trap, like quicksand for the spirit and soul.

Some mornings, I raced to see if I could thank Him for a hundred things without stopping. I was thankful for transcendent things, such as the blood of Jesus. In the next breath, I thanked Him for the rich smell of coffee and the mug's warmth in my hands. I thanked Him for the assurance of eternal life and for the way my yellow lab wagged her tail whenever I came into the room, for forgiveness, popcorn, the Holy Spirit, the summer breeze, the promises of God, and being able to see the mountains from my street. To an eavesdropper, it might have seemed as if my thankful heart had no direction, but it did—it all went upward. *Thank you, Jesus, for everything*. A grateful heart kept depression at bay.

Dr. Carole Leaf, a cognitive neuroscientist, recently posted a link, *Thankfulness and Mental Health,* which included the following observation: "Gratitude is such a powerful thing! When you have a grateful attitude, your brain releases neurotransmitters and neuro-hormones that will boost mood, focus, clear thinking and activate a flow of healthy quantum energy through the brain and body, enhancing mental and physical health. So next time you are anxious, find something to be grateful for!" (Dr. Caroline Leaf, *Facebook,* June 10, 2018)

It was as if my gratitude headed depression off at the pass. I didn't know that deep grief often opens the door to depression, resulting in brain chemistry changes so significant that they rewire the brain. As you give thanks, you control your brain chemistry, forcing it to produce feel-good neurotransmitters, thus healing your emotions. No wonder the Bible tells us to give thanks in all things.

I have a friend who had come to the Lord after several years of a tumultuous marriage and no longer loved her husband. She admitted she actually hated him. A Christian woman told her she should make a list of all of her husband's good points and go through that list every morning, thanking God for her husband's good qualities. Since she had met Jesus in a real way, she was willing to do anything she was told to help her grow in her Christian life and please the Lord. So, she took a pen and paper and sat down to try to write a list. She stared at that paper for a long time. "Lord, there is nothing good about him. Show me *one* thing, and I will thank you for it."

"He works," the Lord told her. So, she wrote that down. "I thank God my husband goes to work."

Every morning during her devotions, she would say, "I thank you, God, that my husband works." Without her noticing, after a while, she was saying, "I thank you, God, that my husband works and is not lazy." *Wow*, she thought, *He doesn't just work; he is a hard worker.* Time went by. "Thank you, Lord. My husband works and is not lazy. Thank you that he lets me do what needs to be done with his paycheck." *Amazing.* He didn't nickel and dime her. *Wow*, she had a generous husband. She hadn't realized it. She hadn't seen it before. And the story just gets better from there. As she began to look at her husband with thankfulness, her perspective began to change because gratitude opens our eyes to see how much we have, and it's always more than we ever thought.

I'm not saying some of my days were not a struggle—many days were gloomy, and many weeks were tough. Some days I would fight to stay up. Sara, a dear friend from Portugal, came to visit me during a very dark week. She looked at me and said, "Rebecca, DO NOT fall into depression. It is so hard to climb out once you fall in." I knew she was right, and I knew again that I was not above it, nor did I have the strength in myself to stay out of it.

I stood on the edge of that pit and looked in. It seemed dark and bottomless. One slip and I would be in. One push from the devil's lies on a bad day and I would tumble headlong. I wanted no part of it, and by His grace, I took a small step backward away from its edge, and I did it again with gratitude; step-by-step with thanksgiving, I inched away from darkness.

A thankful heart buoys you up and keeps you from drowning in a sea of sadness and misery; it keeps your eyes open to see the many things that are sweet and beautiful around you. In the midst of the thick fog of shock and despair that tends to blur our vision, a thankful heart sharpens our senses, and we become aware of the blessings that flow from the Father. Not all is darkness, not all is broken, and not all is hopeless.

Gratitude keeps life in perspective: as you thank God for what you have, you are keenly aware of how very much it is, and it prevents you from comparing your life and circumstances to others. Have you noticed how we seldom compare ourselves to those who have it worse than us or have less than we have? We are inclined to measure our prosperity with the richer, our health with the healthier, our intelligence with the gifted, and our overall satisfaction in life with those who seem to have it all.

When we do this, we tend to feel dissatisfied even if we try to cover it up. Our dissatisfaction can quickly turn into envy, and envy colors the way we see life. Discontentment becomes embedded. We become gripers and whiners, and our conversations are peppered with sighs and woeful looks that rotate around what we don't have, who we aren't, and the things we think we will never experience.

If we consistently measure our lives with others, we will always come up on the short end. Life becomes a constant complaint, making us and all of those around us miserable. Someone else will always have a better car, a larger house, a more considerate husband, a more visible ministry, a more exotic vacation, and more successful children to make the ungrateful more ungrateful still. At this point, nothing will look good. Nothing will be fun, and everything will be far from wonderful because, although God's goodness surrounds us, ingratitude hardens our hearts.

On the other hand, when we live in true thankfulness, we can be happy for what others have and even enjoy it with them. Being genuinely grateful and resentful at the same time is impossible. There is no such thing as a grateful griper.

A few weeks after my husband left, a dear friend, remembering that we had gotten married around the same time, cautiously asked me if it would be too difficult for me to attend their 25th wedding anniversary party. They said they would understand if it would be too hard but would love to have me if I felt like I could handle it. Handle it? I would not only handle it, but I would also enjoy their guests, eat the cake, and toast for 25 more happy years. I celebrated their joy, and it did me good.

Gratitude changes resentment into rejoicing. You can be truly delighted for those who have received more, have done better, and gone further. How stupid it would be to allow what I was going through to hinder me from seeing beyond my small universe and from experiencing others' happiness. How many parties have we missed happening all around us? How many celebrations and firework displays have gone unnoticed and un-enjoyed simply because sadness has made us blind and deaf to joy?

A thankful heart opens our eyes to life's beauty, keeps depression and self-pity at bay, and opens a window in the darkness.

CHAPTER 2

Less Than Not Much

'm invited to a lot of weddings and love going to all of them. After the ceremony, while the bride and groom are off trying to capture the moment with the photographer, the rest of us hang around eating hors d'oeuvres, having a drink, and waiting for the banquet. During that time, I casually make my way over to the seating chart and look for my name with the others. There is a slight moment of angst if I don't see it right away.

Am I on it? What if I'm not on the list? Now that would be awkward! Oh good, there's my name; table eight. Cool, next to people I like. Yay! I was invited. Sigh. Relief. There is a place for me.

From the time we start relating to people, we try to find our place and look for our niche. We would love to slip into a spot that's a perfect fit for us, where we are comfortable and, above all, accepted by those important to us. We look for a place where we can breathe easy, let our guard down, and be who we are without sideward glances to see people's reactions to our comments and behavior.

Acceptance and belonging are basic needs for everyone. Every culture and people have rites, regional dress, customs, and celebrations that give them an identity and a secure feeling of being a part of something larger than themselves. No one wants the feeling of being unattached from society or the culture around them; we were made to be part of something bigger, to be connected and comfortable. Even people who want to stick out and be noticed as different usually do it in a trendy sort of way that results in admiration from those who are significant to them, whether they are part of a street gang or part of the jet set.

It's hard to relax when we play the fitting-in game, even though it begins in preschool or wherever you start to mix with the human race. There is usually a self-appointed four year old who marks the beat for your new little world, and you try to follow the tempo like the rest of the gang. Unfortunately, just as you think you know how to march to the beat and sway to the rhythm, either the drummer changes or the meter changes, and you lose your spot in the parade.

As we mature, we recognize that the whole acceptance game is superficial and has to do with what we own, what we look like, and what we can do, and we recognize that the idea is absurd. Material possessions, height or skill, don't increase one's worth—we know that—but we get drawn into it over and over and over, and it is hard to break the cycle that started way back when, when we felt measured, evaluated, and didn't

12

make the cut. At least that's the impression we got. Oh, the need to belong! It pushes us to care about things we never thought would be important to us.

I embarrassed myself not long ago, and was able to laugh out loud about it, but it showed me that I am as pathetic as everyone else. Although I have self-righteously prided myself in being above the "I have to own this to be cool" and the "I have to shop there to be respected," I realized that I was as needy as everyone else.

I was shopping with my friend Jeannie at her favorite second-hand store and found a hardly-used designer purse for fifty bucks. I had never had one, and seriously, cross my heart, had never ever wanted one, but I bought it. It was pink, gold, and pretty. When I got back to the house, I put it on my shoulder and looked in the mirror and immediately felt an elevated sense of self-esteem. I was shocked and amused and wondered what in the world I would feel like if I drove an expensive upscale car. Would I feel more valuable, worth more than before?

How we would love to live unencumbered by the trend of the moment, the opinion of others, and the need to feel a part of what's happening. Wouldn't it be great if we were so secure in who God is and who He has made us that having certain things, being included or being welcomed in the right places, would add nothing at all to the way we feel about ourselves?

We would not have to impress; we would not have to pretend, and best of all, we would not have the mild anxiety that most of us live with, feeling that we don't measure up and never will.

The problem is that we never get to the place where we settle comfortably into the easy chair of self-approval. It only takes a quick comparative glance at our life and someone else's to show us that we lag behind. In my experience with people, the more some excel at something, the worse they feel about themselves. After the initial high of landing the big job, getting the scholarship, being recorded, or winning the medal, anxiety sets in. No longer a part of the masses, they now compare themselves with the talented elite.

I'm still surprised when I talk to intelligent, talented, or beautiful people who *never* seem to feel they can get APPROVED stamped on their forehead and come to a place where they finally accept themselves, relax and rest in their souls.

Most of us live, day in and day out, doing the best we can, never happy with the end result, wishing we would try a little harder, and feeling that if people really knew us, they would be extremely disappointed in us. After all, *we* are. I would suggest that the focus on goals, improvement, and self-esteem have done the opposite of what many of the self-help books had intended. The more we work on ourselves, the more inept we seem, and try as we may, we just don't feel new and improved, even after all the invested effort. Could we be going about the whole thing backwards?

After a meeting a few months ago, a woman came up to me for prayer. She said, "Could you pray for me? I lack self-esteem, and I just don't feel like much." Her head was down and her eyes were closed, waiting for a prayer that would make her feel better, more valuable, and accepted.

"Do you know why you don't feel like much?" I asked her, and paused for the question to hang in the air for a few seconds. "You don't feel like much, because you aren't much." I let it sink in a moment. "You aren't much, and I'm not much, and none of us are much, and that is why we need Jesus. He is much, and we can be a part of who He is."

She opened her tightly-shut eyes, looked at me, and broke into a smile. She was so relieved to find out that she could just be small and insecure. She didn't have to fix herself, improve herself, or even like herself. She could get to know the One who is everything, who is all in all. Her worth will skyrocket when it comes from His love and His friendship.

The truth is none of us have a lot to offer, and when we realize we don't have to impress ourselves or others, it is liberating. I continued to talk to this precious woman, someone who had been beaten down by the words and actions of others, and encouraged her to get to know the God who loved her unconditionally.

When we focus on the One who doesn't judge on outward appearance, intelligence, or talent, and whose love is constant and unchanging, we become the most secure people in the universe. We are comfortable in our own skin and don't have to look around and compare ourselves to anyone else because we are truly loved, we are truly liked, and what matters to God is the realization that without Him, we are "not much."

Many years ago, my friend Nancy shared a message at our church about Mephibosheth and David that I never forgot. Mephibosheth was a man who was crippled because of an incident he had nothing to do with and had no control over. His family was fleeing a life and death situation brought on by the mistakes and sins of his grandfather Saul.

Bless little Mephibosheth's heart! His nanny, the very person who was supposed to be keeping him safe, lost her grip on him and hurt him forever. She didn't mean to. She was running for safety, trying to save herself and him, but in the chaos and panic—trying to carry more than just a baby—she dropped him and he became disfigured forever. Maybe he hurt when he walked, hurt when he sat; maybe he hurt all the time. It's not clear in this passage if he dragged himself along, was carried, or just had an awkward limp, but the emotional pain of his handicap ran much deeper and was more severe than any physical injury he had experienced.

He was orphaned, poor, and deformed, and none of it was his fault. I doubt that he ever awoke with a sense of hope, believing things would improve and that, perhaps, life would get better. After all, he was less than "not much."

Not far from where Mephibosheth woke up every day, King David had been thinking about his deceased friend Jonathan and missing him. Have you ever lost someone and wanted to hang out with his or her family just to feel close to them, even though you really didn't know them? You might have them over, even though you never did before, and search for your lost friend's smile in the faces of their kids or grandkids. Perhaps this is what happened to David. As he thought about the past and began to go over the slaughter of Jonathan's family in his mind, he wondered if maybe someone had survived, and if they had, he would love to honor his friendship with Jonathan by being kind to them and be comforted by their nearness. This is how Samuel tells the story:

The king asked, "Is there no one still alive from the house of Saul to whom I can show God's kindness?"

Ziba answered the king, "There is still a son of Jonathan; he is lame in both feet."

"Where is he?" the king asked.

Ziba answered, "He is at the house of Makir son of Ammiel in Lo Debar."

So, King David had him brought from Lo Debar, from the house of Makir son of Ammiel. When Mephibosheth, son of Jonathan, the son of Saul, came to David, he bowed down to pay him honor.

David said, "Mephibosheth!"

"At your service," he replied.

"Don't be afraid," David said to him, "for I will surely show you kindness for the sake of your father Jonathan. I will restore to you all the land that belonged to your grandfather Saul, and you will always eat at my table."

Mephibosheth bowed down and said, "What is your servant, that you should notice a dead dog like me?" (2 Samuel 9:3-9)

David paid no attention to Mephibosheth's opinion of himself. All he wanted was to have one of Jonathan's children close. David welcomed Mephibosheth at his table, not because of what he had accomplished or because of what he owned, but because of who his father was and because of the covenant of friendship he had made with him.

So many unexpected things happened to Mephibosheth that day. He went from being a poor man who had lost his inheritance, to a wealthy landowner with crops and servants. But more important than what he now owned was the surprising invitation he received to have fellowship with the king. He could hobble over to the palace crippled but invited, flawed but welcomed, handicapped but loved. And when he sat down for the meal with the king and other fine people, his twisted feet would be hidden under the table. He was in a place where he was welcomed, accepted, and received.

Just as David welcomed Mephibosheth, King Jesus gives us an open invitation to His table. It is a place of nourishment, refreshment, and fellowship. Not all of us accept it, because we have that same "dead dog" feeling that Mephibosheth used to describe himself, and only look on from afar, never accepting what He so freely offers. It's a come as you are, come as you feel, come hungry invitation, but still, we wait; we think about it. We wonder if perhaps there is a table in the kitchen somewhere: where the "not much" people can sit next to the "dead dog" people, where it's a little bit darker, so the damage deep down in our souls isn't as visible and no one will notice that we are those people who were orphaned, dropped, lost their inheritance, and have never fully recovered.

But there's not a second table near the back of the room. There's only one and it is bathed in light. There is a place card with your name on it, there's one with mine, and the host has paid a dear price for our invitation—we belong there.

We can limp into the dining room and over to the banquet He has prepared for us. We can lay our crutches down, find our place, and scoot our chair up to the table of acceptance where our flaws are covered; our accidents are forgotten, our mistakes don't matter, and our twistedness is concealed. It is there that we can take a deep breath, rest, and recover from dragging lifeless limbs around.

The invitation to feast at the table with King Jesus is an open one. We don't arrive to crash the party. We have received a personal, engraved invitation: engraved on the palms of His hands, signed in His blood, and personally delivered. Let's accept it.

CHAPTER 3

Fragile Packaging

Have you ever received a gift in a box that something else originally came in? You could unwrap an iPad box, open it, and find a book inside, or open a ring box from a jewelry store to find hand-made earrings. Talk about a letdown! The exact opposite is true of us, though.

We are ordinary and average containers, yet have a beautiful gift inside. All the riches of Christ have been deposited in our hearts. How often I have to remind myself of the treasure I hold, especially in this world of comparison, fake advertising, and self-improvement. If I forget the package is supposed to be common and perishable, I quickly fall back into giving myself new orders, new goals, and new kicks in the seat of the pants to spiff myself up; yet it's not the wrapping but the gift inside that is meant to shine.

As far back as I can remember, I've had a little drill sergeant inside my head yelling orders. But even he gets discouraged because although he yells "forward march" to new destinations and toward new goals, this soldier gets tired, bored, distracted, and wanders off the trail. Sometimes, I just turn around and go back to the barracks where I started, always accompanied by condemnation and discouragement. Since I know I'm not supposed to live condemning myself, I square my shoulders once again, hold my head high, and try to walk confidently being "just me." However, I soon get tense because the real question is, do I really want to be just me?

I swing back and forth. One minute, I tell myself, *just relax, God made you and accepts you as you are. Enjoy Him, enjoy the people you love and enjoy life.* The next minute, I'm thinking that if I relax too much, I'll never change at all and will always be the same flawed and imperfect person in the same old flimsy container. And I don't really want that. So, I snap the whip and get myself marching to the drumbeat of "you could be better, you could do better, try a little harder, for heaven's sake."

And of course, I could be better. You could too. But lasting self-improvement is not easy for most of us. Countless books, both Christian and secular, give us tips and steps to be a better version of ourselves. I don't discard them entirely. Some do have some great hacks that have helped me. But even if I organize my life better, keep track of my emails, and go to the gym, I still fight the underlying feeling of failure.

Supposing I get my closet under control. There is still more junk hanging out of the drawers of my life making me feel unsightly to others when they get close to me. Perhaps I could organize the present junk drawers of my life, yet there would still be boxes that I haven't dealt with for years, stacked in a messy manner in the garage of my personality and memory.

I'd love to say I have eliminated the tension between "relax, this is the way God made you" and "if I don't get with it and change myself, I will be like this forever." I know that God loves me just the way I am and His grace covers me, but I don't always like myself that much and certainly don't want to stay the same forever. Thus, the pendulum swings back and forth.

The emphasis I have placed on self-improvement has varied throughout the stages of life and so has the frustration of never quite making the mark. Although less now than in the past, not making the grade and underachieving has become my sleeping dragon. I often feel it snoozing nearby and hear its breathing, in and out, in and out, "You could do better; you could be better."

I do a pretty good job of ignoring it most of the time. I defend myself from its breath with my shield of faith, all Christ has done for me on the Cross, and my position in Him. But it keeps one sleepy eye open, watching for an opportunity to roar and scorch me with the flick of its fiery dragon breath. The heat sends me scurrying back to my fortress of good works where I strive to read more and surf the web less, cook more and snack less, do things of lasting value and goof off less. Pray. Don't complain. And above all, just be a nicer person.

At this point in my life, I should be able to say that I have slain the dragon of striving and personal effort. But actually, I have learned to live with him. After all, if he wasn't around, I might throw myself in front of YouTube forever, never call my mother, and "let the world go to hell in a handbasket," as they say. So when I get too relaxed and happy, I slip into my dragon's cave and shake him out of hibernation.

Do your job! Don't you see, I'm having a little too much fun in life? Roar at me, scare me into productivity and make me shake a leg. I need to accomplish something I can see, others can appreciate, and God can smile down upon.

Oddly enough, my trips to the dragon cave never seem to shake me into consistent action, rather, they tend to wear me out and discourage me. The dread of not amounting to much seldom results in lasting change. Keeping the momentum up is impossible because, in the end, I know, my dragon will never really eat me. Sigh.

One New Year's Day, when contemplating a list of resolutions, I went back to my journal and realized the previous year's goals would work fine since nothing had altered all that much. My weaknesses were still weak. My tone of voice was still harsh. My flaws were apparent and totally exposed for the world to see and my desire for things to be different remained a desire which had never materialized into visible growth.

That New Year's morning, I tried to quiet the voices in my head and heart and listen to Him. "It's not what you do, it's who you are," came the memory from somewhere, spoken by someone in my past. "Your being affects your doing."

As I sat with my list in my lap, I reminded myself once more that He is the one who transforms our hearts, and as our hearts are transformed, we see what is important to Him. He is the gift that we have in these fragile boxes, and when we receive from Him, He shines out, just as the apostle Paul writes: "For God, who said, 'Let light shine out of darkness,' made his light shine in our hearts to give us the light of the knowledge of God's glory displayed in the face of Christ. But we have this treasure in jars of clay to show that this all-surpassing power is from God and not from us." (2 Corinthians 4:6-7) *The Living Bible* translation says, "This makes it clear that our great power is from God, not from ourselves."

The treasure that we hold is powerful, mighty to heal, to transform, and mold us, so the knowledge of who He is can shine from us. He is so much bigger than anything we could ever be; the "all-surpassing power" coming from a divine source should be obvious to both us and the world. The all-surpassing power belongs to God and not to us. He offers to fill our fragile selves with all that He is and we relax, knowing that as we yield ourselves to Him, He promises transformation by His Spirit.

This is good news. This is great news. Because of the fact that we are made of clay, we relax and rely on the power we carry. It's not *in spite* of our frailty but *because* of it.

Being a self-made man is a concept admired in our culture and society, yet it's the opposite of what God designed. He designed a weak and needy people whose only hope was a Savior outside of themselves. Try as we may, try as we might, we were created to crash and burn unless connected to the source of the all-surpassing power that flows from being a child of God.

The psalmist was aware of this fact and expressed it well in Psalm 103:14, as he reminded himself that God knows his flawed state: "For he knows how we are formed, he remembers that we are dust." He knows. He remembers.

This is freeing. Not only do we not have to feel strong, intelligent, or powerful—we aren't supposed to. I am never frustrated when I am walking in the awareness of my vulnerability and "dustiness", holding onto God and all His promises for dear life. When I forget and think I need to get it together and be in control, my stress level goes off the charts and I stumble over my faulty fortitude. We are aware that we need God for the big stuff, but we try to do everyday life on our own.

Surely, we can handle the daily routine, right? But we need to rely on the treasure we hold even more in the daily grind. The light of the glory of the knowledge of Christ can shine into the monotony of the nine-to-five, the soccer practice, or a long commute.

When we are aware of how human we are and that it's OK to be average, we can lay all our frustrations with ourselves at His feet. We can rest in who and what He wants us to be. We can settle in our hearts what it is that He is asking of us, and walk with our hand in His, allowing His power to do the work.

He offers to fill our earthen vessel with all He is. We do the yielding, He does the transformation by his Spirit. This is good news. This is great news. We are made of clay and can relax because our power comes from the knowledge of all Jesus has done for us, and not from our own human efforts.

I know myself so well, I am surprised that God could be glorified in any way in my life. His treasure is held in a container, far from perfect, scatter-brained, and easily distracted. It would rather have chats and a cup of coffee than do hard work any day. It gets rattled and nervous. Sometimes it is afraid. Sometimes its faith is weak and doubt grows. It can even sin, envy, gossip, or judge, and then wonder, "How can you still be here? Don't you get tired of me?" Yet, the treasure doesn't slip away. He stays. He abides and transforms from the inside out. He knows. He remembers. He remembers I am but dust.

Our priceless Savior has taken up permanent residence in the hearts of our human vessel, and it doesn't matter if we feel worthy of it or not. He is here to stay. We might be sad, full of doubt, or frustration, but we still hold the treasure, and His power will shine forth. The shape, the color, the size, or the vintage of the jar is of no consequence.

We will always be ordinary and never worthy of His presence within us, no matter how much we straighten up, improve, and get it all together. The treasure is far too precious. We are far too human. We hold the Creator in our heart—we, the created, hold the Creator, and that is too amazing and beautiful for words.

CHAPTER 4

The Clothes Hamper

I worked in *die Wäsherei* or laundry room at a Bible school in Northern Germany when I was twenty. Students would leave their dirty clothes outside their doors to be picked up, washed, dried, folded, and left on shelves labeled with their names. The laundry system at the school changed a few years after I left, and they installed a laundromat where students could take care of their own clothes, but while I was there, the laundry was a communal affair.

Part of the process was redemptive, in a way. The clothes and sheets showed up rumpled and smelly and returned folded and fresh. There is always a sense of satisfaction when something comes in one way and goes out new and improved, but it didn't take me long to realize I was getting to know students in ways most people didn't, and that I had never wanted to.

I tried not to think about the people whose clothes I was doing, but that was impossible, for I folded even their underwear. Yes, underwear. I remember the first time I did it too. It made me think beneath the surface, even if I tried not to.

The girl who wore a jean skirt and the same sweater every day, had pretty matching undergarments beneath the simple exterior. The guy who never smiled wore bumblebee jockey shorts. The fancy chick wore white cotton—fancy on the outside and comfy on the inside. Then there was the guy whose folded clothes never included undies. I told myself perhaps he liked to hand wash his personals, but I knew I was kidding myself. There are times when you should not leave things to your imagination.

There is so much that others don't know about us—things unmentionable, under layers of outerwear—that if people knew, they could be smiling and chatting with us while secretly being repulsed by us.

My favorite stylish friend once told me she felt hypocritical if she matched outside and not underneath. She said she felt inconsistent. It would be nice to know you look good underneath the surface all the time, but most of us can't keep it up. Even if we buy matching sets, after a few weeks or less, the pink bottoms aren't with the pink tops anymore, and we end up wearing new and old, fresh and ratty, lacy and plain Jane, all mixed up together.

Of course, in the big scheme of life, underwear doesn't matter, but the metaphor of consistency does sound nice. As one of my aunts used to say, "You could unexpectedly end up in the hospital, and you would not want the doctors and nurses to be appalled at your undergarments." I suppose we could push that over into the spiritual and say if we were ever exposed unexpectedly, we would like what has been hidden from view to match what everyone has seen openly.

I once went to speak at a women's conference, and my suitcase didn't arrive with me. It's common knowledge you should take a change of clothes, pajamas, and toothbrush in your carry-on, just in case, but I never did. I thought the odds of my bags being on my flight were on my side, but not this time. Since there was only one flight a day from my city, I knew my bag wouldn't arrive before the morning sessions. There I was, in a place I'd never been, with people who had never met me, prepared to speak to an auditorium full of women, and I was looking like "something the cat drug in," as my grandmother used to say.

The women who picked me up at the airport and waited for my suitcase with me were so kind. When my bag didn't arrive, they wanted to take me shopping, but I told them some pajamas and a toothbrush would suffice for the night. The thought of trying to find something to wear under pressure was worse than looking a mess. So, I spoke twice, all wrinkled and frumpy; once on the joy of our salvation and once on the peace that passes all understanding. We ate lunch and went to the hotel where my bag was waiting for me. Yay!

It was a good conference. I loved being there; I liked my translator and enjoyed teaching the ladies. When the conference was over, some of the women in leadership came to the front to say a few words. The one who had picked me up at the airport said something like this, "I have been impressed with our speaker because she lives her message. Yesterday, her suitcase didn't arrive, and she faced a conference with no clean clothes, makeup, or her things, yet she didn't lose her joy, and she was very peaceful about the whole thing. So, she has a right to speak about peace and joy." Wow. Even *I* was impressed with myself, but mainly because I hadn't even thought about it. It was my natural reaction, and it made me feel like my spiritual underwear matched. Ha.

We are emotionally healthy when what others observe on the outside and what we feel on the inside is pretty much the same. Our goal is for pretension and posing to get chipped away little by little until what people see is what they get. My aunt's advice about not shocking the ambulance driver with ratty underwear is good counsel. If there were an emergency, a moment of unexpected exposure, we would not want to be embarrassed by what people see.

I have seen so many people react under pressure in ways that reveal what they profess to believe on the outside is also real deep down. My friend had a co-worker in our office who accidentally erased seven years of photographs on her computer. The woman shouldn't even have been at her desk in the first place, and no, they weren't backed up. My friend was upset, but not at the person who did it. She took a deep breath, forgave her, and went on. Her reputation in the office suddenly went through the roof. Someone ironically said, "She acts like a Christian." I say ironically because we were all in the ministry and supposedly lived like Christians every day, yet when someone *actually did,* we were impressed.

Then there was the time when two friends' children got into a brawl that turned violent. One could have been seriously injured, yet his parents' reaction was one of comfort and understanding toward the other one's parents and vice versa. "They are real Christians," people said. Our goal, our heart's desire, is that our automatic reaction and retort reflect the One we claim to love. We would love for others to call us *real* Christians.

Returning to the illustration of the laundry room, let's consider the soiled laundry of the past we hope no one ever sees, ours and others'. What do we do when we discover there are things our friends keep hidden so people won't change the way they think about them? And what about our own dark secrets? Perhaps years of friendship go by and then you find out about the attempted suicide, the abortion they had, the child they gave up for adoption, or the fatal accident they had while drunk. There is so much classified information, undisclosed and unpublished beneath the put-together exteriors. There are so many secrets stuck in the bottom of the hamper.

I was having lunch with a woman who had been in prostitution. It is her secret. It is the thing that would change how people think about her, talk to her, or look at her if they only knew. It is her shame when she takes her eyes off Jesus who has forgiven and forgotten. Now, it is covered up by a good job, a family, and a life remade by the restorer of all things. And yet, there is the underlying fear her past just might make it to the Bible school laundry room. And then, what would people think?

Hearing people's secrets should create patience in us instead of judgment. We could whisper to ourselves, "Oh, so that's why she is so afraid," or "So that is why he is so insecure—oh," and increase our patience toward all people.

People carry such shame. Often, it is shame about what they have done, and other times, it's shame about what the unfair circumstances of life have done to them. They carry guilt about things they feel they could have avoided; guilt about the "what if I had only?" or "only hadn't?"; remorse about decisions made and opportunities lost.

Experiencing divorce while in ministry has forced me to look shame in the face and decide what to do with it. Sometimes it wants to take over, but never because I don't feel loved, accepted, and forgiven by God. The fear of opinions and the fear of man tempts me to hang my head and feel *less than*. I'm the same person who runs straight up to the throne of grace with no hesitation, yet tends to stop and think a minute before she walks through other doors and into other groups of people. I fear I will perceive the "it-takes-two-to-tango" look or the silent implication "there are *two sides to every story.*" If judged, I would not come out unscathed, but I can square my shoulders and hold my head high because of Him. Because of my shame-bearer, I can walk through every door and into any crowd.

Shame pops up at odd times in life. I was in a Christian leadership meeting a few years back. It was a mostly-men meeting, which already has an element of that *you're-less-than* feeling and *what right do you have to be here*? It's stupid to feel that way, but it's a lie that sometimes seeps in under the door of my self-worth and tries to take up residence in my redeemed heart. It tries to convince me that I don't belong in places. At this particular meeting, I was battling with this accusation from the enemy and feeling out of place.

The speaker was great. He lifted my spirits, inspired me to love God more, and I clapped enthusiastically with the rest of the crowd. When he came down off the platform and headed out, his wife slid out of her seat to exit with him, they linked pinkies and out they went. Most people didn't even notice the linking of the pinkies or think twice about their departure. This wouldn't have mattered to anyone, but when I saw it, the devil told me, "*You* failed your minister husband; *you* could have saved him. Shame, shame, shame on you." Oh, how the devil taunts us. At those times, we must take a deep breath and remember whose we are and who has wiped away our past with His shed blood.

The enemy would like us to go through our cleaned and pressed closet to convince us our garments need to go back to the cleaners. He likes to remind us of stains that have been removed once and forever, and he tries to convince us the costly and precious robe of righteousness isn't really our size. Actually, it was purchased with us in mind and was tailor-made, a perfect fit.

We're told not to air our dirty laundry in public, but if we have received the forgiveness and healing He offers, we don't have any to air. In *The Message* version of Psalm 51:7, we read, "Soak me in your laundry, and I'll come out clean, scrub me, and I'll have a snow-white life."

We must accept this news for ourselves and for others. When we are able to accept, and not reject, it makes it easier for people to be themselves around us. They don't have to fake it to gain our approval and be liked. We need to lower the bar for acceptance, not raise it. We should get comfortable in our robe of righteousness and wear it with pride in the One who generously gave it to us. We know it is a one-size-fits-all—it fits us and it fits others. It's always clean and always new.

CHAPTER 5

The Best and Worst Part of Life

Has anyone made it through parenthood without accidentally physically hurting your child? I didn't realize that my son wasn't out of the car all the way and slammed the car door on his eight-year-old finger. Although it was a minor injury and healed pretty quickly, I can remember the guilt of not being careful with someone so important to me.

That was many years ago, but I hurt someone else recently, not with the car door on their finger but deep in their soul. It could be the end of our friendship, although I hope not. It's not worth going into the "he said, I said, she said, they said" of it all, but I do look back and wonder how it could have been avoided, especially the part I played in the breakdown. There's nothing like hurting someone you love, being misunderstood, and then being accused of doing it on purpose. Not fun.

We end up doing things that affect the lives of others in negative ways without ever wanting to, and although most misunderstandings can be fixed with a sincere apology, others deteriorate to a place where a once valued relationship completely disappears out of your life. *How many have I loved and lost?* I've wondered.

It's even worse when you planned steps of loving confrontation and went through a kind conversation in your mind beforehand, and it STILL went south. I hate it, and I hate the feeling in the pit of my stomach after it happens. I hate going over and over it, wondering at what point I went wrong and what I could have done to have avoided it. You've heard that hindsight is 20/20. Well, it's not. Sometimes I look back, and the past is as foggy as it was when it was the present. I still have no idea how things got so bad.

Relationships: the best and the worst part of life.

We weren't meant to do life on our own, but can understand those who end up living with two dogs, three cats, and one parrot. There are days when most of us envy the guy who builds a cabin in the woods so he won't have to deal with people. I think we've all been tempted with the thought of a silent monastery somewhere, where it's against the rules to talk or make eye contact. Life might be more comfortable that way.

But God said, "Adam, you need a friend, it's not good to be by yourself" (paraphrase, Gen. 2:18). Adam lived in Paradise at the time. Eden was a pure, unadulterated utopia. He walked and talked with the God of the universe in a landscape of perfect harmony, but his very creator told him that he needed someone like himself in his ideal life. Isn't that something! The eternal God who is big enough to satisfy every longing sets us among human beings to "do life with." He surrounds us with people to give to and receive from, to teach and learn from, to love and be loved by, and to forgive and receive forgiveness.

King Solomon says if one is alone in the bed he gets chilly. If one takes a tumble, he needs help getting up. We all need a warm soul and a helping hand on a daily basis (paraphrase, Ecclesiastes 4:10,11).

So why is it so hard to keep friendships warm and cozy? Why is it so hard to know when someone has stumbled and why so hard to pick them up? It's even worse when you are the one (hopefully by accident) who pulled the blankets off the other one and left them shivering, uncovered, with teeth chattering. Or the time you did the opposite of helping someone up, tripping them instead.

That's what I'm feeling right now. I feel like instead of helping someone I love, I left them cold and fallen, all because of a string of stupid mistakes. And who knows if it can ever be repaired.

Why did I even address the issue? Why didn't I just ignore it, turn a blind eye, smooth things over, or make a superficial excuse?

The reason is that I want to live in truth, but the outcome of loving confrontation isn't always healing, and it is the reason we avoid conflict at all cost and keep our walls of defense high and thick. Being vulnerable sounds noble, but the results can be messy, which is why we just prefer to create our own little monasteries. In the midst of a multitude of acquaintances and relationships, we make a vow of silence and try to keep our mouths shut and our eyes fixed straight ahead, lest what we say ruffles feathers or makes waves, causing the outcome to be worse than the initial problem.

I grew up in a home that confused love with communication, and peace with ignoring conflict. It was a place where love covered a multitude of sins, so if you were hurt, you extended loving forgiveness, or if you were the offending party, you apologized, never to mention it again. The idea of working things through to an understanding of what really happened or why it hurt was out of our circle of comprehension.

There was an unwritten rule that if you loved the person, there was no need ever to bring it up again, even if there was an open wound of misunderstanding and confusion. There was a secret hope that if you ignored it long enough, it would go away. But, of course, it didn't. It was swept under the rug, only to resurface later, adding another layer to the complicated communication of communal living. There are things that a hug can't fix.

Much has been written about what to do when someone hurts or offends you. But what about when you are the offending party? And what if the offended one doesn't believe your side of the story because trust has been broken? Oh, sigh. At this point, all I can do is leave it in God's hands, hope that time will heal, and trust that His grace will travel to the places in the heart where my detailed explanations and heartfelt apologies don't reach.

With every misunderstanding comes the temptation to shut your heart up and tread softly around difficult issues in life. The only problem with this is that we begin to live tiny little lives that only encompass "us four and no more." The fewer people we know, the fewer people we open up to, the less opportunity to be hurt and to hurt others. But I don't want my life to be so small and my heart so shrunken that no one fits but my kids and me. It wasn't why I was created, it wasn't why I was rescued, and it doesn't reflect my Savior.

Being vulnerable sounds noble, but it is risky, and if we don't keep our eyes on Jesus, our example, we begin to shut out anyone who makes us uncomfortable, who thinks differently than we do.

I've come to people to try to explain why I am upset or to understand their reaction or thought process, thinking that because I am being vulnerable, loving, and sincere, they will drop all defenses and we can figure things out. Sometimes the outcome of the conversation is comprehension, acceptance, and joy, but not always. And it goes both ways. How many people have wished I'd understood them and I haven't? Maybe I tried, maybe I didn't. Perhaps I even treated their hurt carelessly, brushed them aside and thought that their pain was uncalled for, a sign of immaturity. The first step to understanding people is wanting to.

Not long ago a young friend was complaining about a woman she felt was difficult. I asked her, "Did you know she escaped slavery in her country?" and I proceeded to give her a couple of details about what she had been through. Of course, my friend had no idea and felt terrible about her quick judgment and lack of patience. Wouldn't it be wonderful if we could be accepting of people without knowing the details of their past?

Our example is Jesus again. Read this verse: "For we do not have a high priest who is unable to feel sympathy for our weaknesses, but we have one who has been tempted in every way, just as we are—yet he did not sin." (Hebrews 4:15).

Jesus. Oh, to be like Him. Although He never fell into any sin that we are tempted with, He is able to understand why we are tempted and feels for us. He understands why we want to shut and bolt the door of our hearts. He was despised and rejected, a man who has suffered sorrow and knew what grief was all about, so He understands. He gets it.

We can't always fix everything, but we can keep our hearts soft. The apostle Paul said, "If it is possible, as far as it depends on you, live at peace with everyone" (Rom. 12:18). I think Paul was saying, use all your power to make things right. Take all the steps you can toward the offended, someone who is estranged and angry with you. If what you give is not enough for them, it's enough for God, and you can be at rest.

CHAPTER 6

Ágata

I was walking beside a river late one spring. Very few flowers were left on the wild almond trees in central Spain, but the rosemary was in bloom, and wild thyme was flowering everywhere. The wheat was up a few inches, and the olive trees, always silver green. I had been to a memorial service the night before; maybe that is why everything looked so clear and bright. There's nothing like a funeral of someone in their 40's to uncloud your vision and cause you to reflect on life and on the person who is now gone.

Not many had attended the service, but there were more than I had expected—a random bunch at best—all belonging to different groups of people who had known our friend. She had been a frustration to me because she hadn't seemed to have her feet on the ground and I was always trying to plant them solidly there for her.

"You need to get a real job," I would say. "You need to make a home. You need to have a schedule and not wake up every morning and go wherever the wind blows you."

She didn't really live anywhere. She "couch-surfed" long before anyone had coined a term for sleeping in someone's living room for free. When I heard she was terminally ill, I wondered if anyone would take care of her. She had no one. She was alone in the world—or so I thought. Then, I heard that she was staying with a friend, and another friend had moved in to help care for her. A few months later, someone had rented her a room, and someone else lived with her in case she needed anything. There was a Peruvian woman who dropped in on her and a Dutch couple who was taking her to her appointments.

That night at the memorial, I counted about ten nationalities among the thirty or so people who brought food and music. Someone had made a slideshow. People said kind words about her giving heart. "She gave good advice." "She was full of wisdom." "You were always welcome to anything she had." Six people from Ecuador sang a song in Quichua in gratitude for her generosity. She had owned a keyboard, and she had loaned it to them. "It was so, so heavy," one of the men said. And then they all laughed, remembering her dragging her piano around everywhere.

She was not a frustrating memory for them. I had obviously missed what some had seen and received. I had seen a disorganized, unconventional life—no house, no permanent job, and no future. I tried to bring her down to earth, to settle her down, but she didn't want to settle the way I thought settling should be. So I gave up on her and moved on to more rational relationships. And she, she moved on to others also— friends who let her sleep on their sofas, wanted her advice, and played her piano.

How much do we miss because we are taken aback when people don't fit into our mold of normal? Maybe their outward appearance or behavior doesn't meet our standard and we can only receive from a person we consider put together. We judge, you know. We all do it. We write people off before we give them a chance to write something valuable on our hearts.

I have many embarrassing examples of snap judgments, but I'll share the worst one. I saw a woman come into a conference who didn't go with the flow; she didn't submit to the schedule, she came in late and left early. *What's wrong with her?* I wondered. She seems odd, strange. I really am almost too embarrassed to write this, but the woman wasn't strange; she was deaf. Of course she didn't go with the flow; she couldn't hear the flow! Oh, my.

We get it so, so wrong, so much of the time. I got to know her and loved her. She loved the Word. She loved her family. Why did I judge her? Why am I drawn to the attractive and successful when I know that what matters is on the inside? I know this, yet prejudice lifts its ugly head from my oh-so-holy heart, and I consider some people of greater value and worth than others. Oh, yuck. I hate myself. I hate myself because I want to get to know some people based only on outward appearance, personal achievement, or charming personality. I hate myself because I am taken aback by deformed faces, poor personal hygiene, ignorance, or mental illness.

Am I so superficial and so unlike Christ that I walk away from those whom Jesus would have walked toward? Jesus, my Lord and example, reached out and touched everyone, even the leper. I would have turned my face away, yet He looked straight at him, conversed with and healed him with His touch. He patted the eyes of a blind man with little mud pies. He must have had to cup his face in one hand and rub gently with the other. Would I have come that close to the blind beggar, or would I have been repelled by his poverty and smell and, perhaps, by the whiteness of his eyes?

When I am repulsed by someone, I am then repulsed by myself and have to look heavenward for help. Knowing who I know and how much He loves us all, I can't afford to allow my personal prejudices to take up permanent residence in my heart because they are the opposite of who He is. I can't coddle them, tolerate them, and excuse them because I am a believer. I am a believer in our glorious Lord Jesus Christ.

In the New Testament, James writes: "My brothers and sisters, believers in our glorious Lord Jesus Christ must not show favoritism. Suppose a man comes into your meeting wearing a gold ring and fine clothes, and a poor man in filthy old clothes also comes in. If you show special attention to the man wearing fine clothes and say, 'Here's a good seat for you,' but say to the poor man, 'You stand there' or 'Sit on the floor at my feet,' have you not discriminated among yourselves and become judges with evil thoughts." (James 2:1-4)

Favoritism sounds softer than prejudice, but it's the same thing, and I guess it has been a problem in the hearts of Christians from the beginning. James was correcting something that was happening in a Christian meeting, inside the building. If there is one place on the face of the earth where people should be seen as equal, it is in church, but even there, we love the rich and the famous, the beautiful and the bright. Way back then, James exhorted the church not to judge people by their great clothes, and we need to hear that exhortation in our hearts every day. James went on to say: "If you really keep the royal law found in Scripture, 'Love your neighbor as yourself,' you are doing right. But if you show favoritism, you sin and are convicted by the law as lawbreakers. For whoever keeps the whole law and yet stumbles at just one point is guilty of breaking all of it." (James 2:8-10).

To paraphrase, James is saying, if you break this one, you break all of them, so stop considering it unimportant and stop making excuses. My heart knows it's not right to rate people, and it knows God is not impressed with outward beauty, bank accounts, status, or IQs. I'm aware there is no prestige in the kingdom of God, and yet I carry a secret scale around. I rate on a scale of one to ten. Just how worthy is this person of my attention?

Let's face it, most of us are average human beings and know we are. So, if we hang with those who are smarter and better-looking, we feel like we are taken up a notch. It's fun to be in cars we'll never own, eat at places we would never go, and walk around with people who act like they own the world we only rent space in. We reject some people because we feel like they are less than us, but love to be with those we think are more than us.

I had a gorgeous young friend named Beatriz and noticed she always got free things and her way about everything. If we were in a bakery, the owner would throw in an extra cookie, or if she knocked on the window of a closed store, they would open up and wait on her. Once when I was with her, I was trying to return something and was being given the run-around. I gave it to her and said, "Hey, you return this for me." She was back in a few minutes with a total refund. *Not fair,* I thought, but was so aware I do the same thing. I often treat people with deference if they are impressive in some way.

I long to see people the way our Lord sees them, but I can't seem to do it on a consistent basis. I need to have the eyes of my heart tweaked. There was a worship song a few years ago, which said, "Open the eyes of my heart, I want to see you, Lord." (Paul Baloche.Integrity Music.1997) But I need to add a verse that says, "Open the eyes of my heart, I want to see people the way you see them, Lord."

At the beginning of Jesus' ministry, He was surrounded by the rich and famous. He was the latest thing happening. He was interesting, and the miracles that He performed were amazing. The bright and the beautiful were attracted to the novelty of His ministry and wanted to be seen with Him. They were impressed by Him, but they were not so impressed by the people He allowed to get close to Him—the sick, the poor, the weak, and the blatant sinners. I've been thinking about the people that Jesus took time with and wonder which ones I would have paid attention to.

- Nicodemus, the Pharisee, member of the Sanhedrin, was intelligent and an interesting conversationalist. I probably would have liked to be with him.

- The rich young leader was loaded, and besides that, he was a good guy. Being his friend would have many advantages like access to a great pool and an invitation to a relaxing summerhouse. Being with someone who was law-abiding and honorable would also be inspiring and morally uplifting.

- The Roman military man, yes, I'd be impressed. A man in uniform! He ordered people around, and I'm impressed by authority.

- Lazarus' house would be fun. Martha was probably an impressive cook and hostess. I like that kind of woman—busy, organized, and hospitable.

But there were others I would easily have ignored, for instance, the short guy in the tree. He, too, was rich like the young leader, but he was anything but law-abiding, and I would have looked down my self-righteous nose at him. Then, there was the corrupt taxman. No one likes a liar and a cheat. I would have written him off as unworthy of more than a superficial hello, but not Jesus. Jesus looked right past behavior and into the heart. He saw the need, the hunger, and the potential of even this corrupt man, and welcomed him into His life as a disciple.

The blind, the lame, the halt, the bright, the rich, and religious: Jesus ran into all of them along the roads and in the villages of Judea, and He loved them all the same. Because He loved them perfectly, He treated them equally. The blind cried out for mercy, the sick reached out and touched Him; the guilty wept and received forgiveness when they encountered our glorious Lord Jesus Christ.

I am encouraged by the story of the blind man in Bethsaida. Some people brought him to Jesus and begged Him to touch their friend. Jesus took his hand in His and led him to the outskirts of town. Then He spit on the man's eyes (weird, I know, but that's the story). He then put His hands on him and asked him if he could see anything. The man replied that he could see better, but people didn't look like people; they looked like trees walking around. So Jesus put His hands on his eyes again. This time, his eyesight was totally restored. He saw everything clearly. The fact that he wasn't made whole when Jesus touched him the first time encourages me.

If the blind man needed more than one touch and Jesus was glad to do it, I can believe my Savior will put His hands on the eyes of my heart again and again until I see men just as He does. Then, nothing will keep me from reaching out and touching them also.

CHAPTER 7

That Selfish Woman

The most selfish person I've ever met was Connie. She lived a couple of blocks from the church, and in all my years of experience with people, I had never known anyone like her.

I met her one day when her sister, who was visiting from out of the country, came to a Sunday service and brought her along. Her sister was a true believer, and as sweet as Connie was awful. She flew transatlantic almost every year to visit her older sister and stayed a few months, concerned at how alone and isolated her sister was.

Naturally, I befriended Connie's sister and began to get to know her a little, and the more time I spent with her, the more she let me in on how complicated it was to live with her sister's extreme selfishness. Connie had taken "it's all about me" up a few notches and was busy perfecting self-absorption.

When summer ended, Connie pressured her sister not to leave her, so she decided to stay longer than planned. The days turned cooler, and she needed a sweater or jacket to keep her warm, and although Connie had a closet full of coats, sweaters, and different wraps, she wouldn't lend one to her sister. The fact that her sister was cold only produced a short lecture on how she should have had more foresight packing, and suggested she call her children and have them send her a sweater, which she did. She wasn't allowed to turn the stove on to heat water for tea, take a warm shower, turn on the heating system, or anything else that might cost a penny.

Had Connie been poor and destitute, her behavior would have been easier to understand. Her house, however, was paid for. She had savings and a great retirement—more than enough to buy her sister several coats, allow her to make warm drinks, keep the house comfortably warm, and care for her every expense.

I hadn't gotten over being repulsed by her selfishness when her sister let me in on another little secret. She told me Connie hadn't taken a bath for many, many weeks; unpleasant, selfish, and now filthy.

She had been a beautiful woman and, even in her eighties, would still have been attractive, had it not been for her hard and mean spirit. Connie told me although she'd had plenty of suitors, she had not gotten married because she didn't want someone in her house all the time. This unwillingness to share her life explained why she hadn't spoken to anyone in her apartment block for years, not even a "hello" in the elevator.

Connie was totally isolated except for the people she saw every day as she went through her routine. She ate lunch at the same little restaurant daily, then took a taxi downtown, drank a Coke at the KFC, and read the paper. She then crossed the main street to a coffee bar for afternoon coffee and cake, bought a magazine to read, and finally took a taxi home in the late evening. She did this every day. She did it alone when her sister wasn't there.

Her sister eventually left, and Connie continued to come to church on Sunday evenings. I decided that I could win this manipulative and awful woman with my love and patience. After all, I was the Superwoman of all things love.

At first, she tried to be civil because it was in her best interest, but she very soon became unbearable. Of all the people I had worked with, Connie was by far the most unpleasant and disagreeable. The more you gave, the more she expected. The nicer you were, the more she demanded. Time spent with her was never enough, and no matter what you did, it wasn't the right thing.

One day, she asked me to go with her to a place downtown where she liked to have her hair done. At eighty-two, it was hard for her to get down there on her own. *This would be the Jesus thing to do*, I told myself. *It can't be that bad. I will even go the second mile; I'll take her to the beauty salon, wait for her, and then have lunch with her.* But the trip was terrible, and I thought the hours would never end. She repeatedly yelled at the hairdresser and got up every ten minutes to be sure I had not left the waiting area. After ordering me not to leave, she reminded me that I had promised lunch. She must have perceived I was ready to bolt.

When I got back to the church a few hours later, all worn and frazzled, someone commended me on my good works. "Wow, I can't believe how patient you are with her."

"Don't congratulate me and don't be fooled," I replied. "I have murder in my heart. I can't stand her. She is mean, hateful, and ungrateful. I want to kill her. *But*...I need her more than she needs me."

I don't remember if it was at the hair-dresser's or in the taxi when I realized that I had never tried to help anyone who had not given back to me, at least a little. This was a first. Maybe people didn't change or heed my counsel, but at least they expressed some sort of appreciation for my time and effort. They usually liked being with me, and their affirmation stroked my self-esteem. And even though the recompense might be small, at the very least, I got coffee out of it. But this was different. There was not enough coffee in Seattle to tempt me to be with this woman. The fact that she was horrible wasn't what was hard for me.

What bothered me, I realized, was that she didn't recognize or appreciate what a kind and giving person I was. In fact, she thought I could stand a lot of improvement and pointed out areas I could work on. She tried to take even more than I offered and didn't admit that she was unworthy of my kindness. This, I realized, was the reason it was difficult for me.

Hey, I am a vibrant young woman with a heavy schedule. You, on the other hand, are old and live at your leisure. Lots of people would love to spend the day with me; no one wants to spend a minute with you. I have tons of friends, and you don't have a friend in the world, yet I am taking the day for you. Therefore, you should recognize it, feel unworthy of it, and above all, make me feel righteous and good by appreciating it and expressing it!

I had no idea what unconditional love was. I had never actually tried to give it until then. We say that we love unconditionally, and I am sure that there are some people who do, but most of us don't. Most of us are never tried to the point of loving without anything in it for us. Even difficult children and impossible spouses tend to have something we need, so we put up with them *unconditionally.*

When I was ready to snap that day at the hair salon, I understood a tiny bit of what God receives from His creation 24/7. He gives and gives. We take and take. He serves. We demand. We pout when we don't get what we want, the way we want it, and served up the way we ordered it. We are, above all, ungrateful. And yet, God keeps loving us perfectly.

We compare ourselves to the Connies of the world and give ourselves little self-righteous pats on the back, instead of comparing ourselves to Christ, who is altogether lovely in His perfection. We need to take a long, hard look at Him, who has no malice, deception, or evil, and be amazed that He looks down upon the likes of us, loves us, and shows us kindness.

Often, when appalled by a Christian's behavior or an evil deed, we measure ourselves by them, shake our self-righteous heads, and say, "I never could have done what they did." And although it sounds religious and oh-so-pious, it's simply not true. We are all capable of extreme selfishness, which always ends in hurt and destruction. We are all capable of grave evil, and the sooner we admit it, the safer we will be.

Overconfidence in one's self is tricky because it looks and feels like strength. We feel tough, but don't realize that we are standing on a slippery slope of pride. One bad day or one weak moment is all it takes to send us sliding. "*I* would *never* do that, and *I* am *incapable* of such behavior." Whoooops!!

There we go, tumbling into that muddy pit we thought we were *way* too holy to ever fall into. "Pride cometh before a fall" proves true once more. Our journey is secure when we recognize that we aren't very strong and that we stand on wobbly legs and unsure footing. If we often doubt our ability to make it to the end without help from above, we'll be OK.

I like the *New Living Translation* of Psalm 10:1: "I waited patiently for the Lord to help me, and he turned to me and heard my cry. He lifted me out of the pit of despair, out of the mud and the mire. He set my feet on solid ground and steadied me as I walked along."

He is the one who lifts us up out of the muck of our failed personal fortitude, sets us on solid ground, and steadies our step. We must recognize our strength comes from Christ and His work alone, or we will become blind to our personal neediness while judging the rest of the world.

Remember the story where the Pharisee and the tax collector were praying in the temple? The Pharisee considered himself holier than the tax collector and pointed out his superiority to God. He even thanked God for being better than the average sinner. "The Pharisee stood and prayed thus with himself, 'God, I thank thee, that I am not as other men are, extortioners, unjust, adulterers, or even as this publican'" (Luke 18: 11).

Meanwhile, the tax collector recognized his need: "And the publican, standing afar off, would not lift up so much as his eyes unto heaven, but smote upon his breast, saying, 'God be merciful to me a sinner'" (Luke 18:13).

Two things are noticeable in this passage. Although the Pharisee starts out being thankful and giving God glory, his prayer quickly degenerates to a self-congratulatory, self-righteous pat on the back while condemning others. Despising people is the result of pride. When he reviewed what he considered the worst sins in his mind, he gave himself an A+ for his conduct.

- Adultery? No.
- Extortion? No.
- Unjust? No.
- Fasting? Yes!
- Tithing? Yes!
- Better than others? Yes! Yes! Yes!

As the Pharisee left the temple, he mistakenly thought God, impressed by his religion, was handing him a trophy and throwing confetti. But he had it all wrong. The opposite was true. According to Jesus, the guy who was ashamed to lift his head, the one who cried for mercy—he's the one that got the prize. The Pharisee needed justification as badly as the tax collector, but he didn't know it. He had deceived himself into believing he didn't need help and thought he had the strength in himself to make the grade.

When we go to the temple to pray, wherever our temple might be—an easy chair in the den, a swing on the porch, or a pew in church—we should ensure we aren't just going through the motions, repeating hollow words and bragging. Neither should we glance around, comparing ourselves to anyone but Christ, lest we end up feeling superior to the one praying alongside. Instead, we should all be beating our breasts, asking for and receiving mercy.

Coming into God's presence and lifting up hands washed in our basin of good works is so human. "I thank thee that I am not like most. I'm better, and if not better, at least I get points for *trying* to be better. And I do thank you that I'm not like Connie, selfish, mean, and smelly. Amen."

Obviously, Connie was appallingly egocentric. Equally appalling, although not as obvious, was my need to feel good about myself and impress others. Both Connie and I were needy. Connie needed a revelation of how her evil heart needed Jesus' redemptive love, and I needed a revelation of how my evil heart needed His redemptive love as well. She needed to repent from her selfish ways. I needed to repent from my dead works and spiritual pride.

She used people to get what she wanted. I used people to get what I needed. She wanted company and someone to help her get around, but I needed someone to stroke my spiritual ego and keep my self-righteousness inflated. Both of us were equally in need of a revelation of God's love and justification.

Try as you may, it's hard to love people when you feel self-righteous because it breeds superiority. If you have pulled yourself up by your own bootstraps, you may have little patience for the person on food stamps, even if you have no idea how they got there or what their story is.

Have your prayers ever sounded like this?

"I thank you, God, I am not like that woman paying with food stamps. I thank you, Jesus, that I wasn't stupid enough to get pregnant at sixteen. I did my homework, got a scholarship, waited for the right man, and am now admired and envied by other women. Thank you, Jesus." Oh, my. Oh, yuck. What a slippery slope this is.

"I thank you, God, that I am not overweight like my friend over there. I thank you I am not undisciplined like she is. I go to *you* instead of the donut shop with *my* anxiety. I recognize that my body is the temple of the Holy Spirit, and the Holy Spirit is not comfortable in size super-huge. I also appreciate how I inherited my parents' skinny genes and that I fit in these skinny jeans. Hallelujah." Thin body—huge, gross, out-of-control pride—if only you could see inside yourself, you would find it disgustingly disgusting.

"I thank you, God, that my children are turning out so well; what a testimony to my good parenting and to doing everything so right. I thank you they aren't like *her* kids, unruly, unkempt, and loud. I never believed a Christian could have a demon, Lord, but sometimes I wonder about her middle one. Thank you, Lord, that I am such a great mother. I can hear you clapping for me, and any moment, my brood will rise and call me blessed. Oh, glory."

You just wait a few more years as you waltz around on the slick ballroom floor of parental pride, and her middle one might start looking extra sweet to you.

All of us could write examples of our self-righteous prayers, the ones we whisper way down deep where no one hears. Wouldn't it be embarrassing if those prayers were prayed out loud over the sound system at a ballpark or someplace? We need to ask God to do that for us. "Lord, blast me with my own words. Let me hear myself." Because when we do, we will "not lift up so much as our eyes unto heaven, but will smite upon our breast, and say, 'God be merciful to me a sinner.'"

The amazing thing is God will be merciful. He showed us great mercy in the sacrifice of Jesus. If He didn't withhold His only begotten son, He will certainly not be deaf to our cry. "Don't give me what I deserve, Lord. Give me a taste of Your unconditional love and kindness."

CHAPTER 8

Oh, That Dream Again

I had a recurring dream for years. In this dream, I was running to catch a mode of transportation with only seconds to spare. I would be running toward the train track just as the train pulled out, or sprinting down the terminal toward my gate, my carry-on falling off my shoulder, my heart pounding, only to arrive at the gate as it was closing. In my dream, I missed the bus, the subway, the train, and the plane.

The only types of transportation that hadn't left without me, in my subconscious, were those I had never ridden—a helicopter, a submarine, a galloping horse or camel—but all the other ways of getting some place I had ever used, I only missed by seconds. This wasn't a nightmare, just a tension dream, and not all that frequent, but often enough for it to become familiar, and I would wake up frustrated, "Oh, that dream, again!"

Then, at a difficult time in my life, I attended an international women's leadership conference. It was many years before the divorce; the kids were small, our ministry was going fairly well, and things should have been fine, but I was desperate. I felt far from God; my passion had turned into pressure, my prayers to rote, and the pages of my Bible brittle and stale. Something needed to happen, or my future looked grim.

During this time, I allowed my thoughts to wander, and I reinvented myself in my mind. Maybe I would do this or do that; maybe I'd go back to school, get a more reasonable job, yet still be a pastor's wife and sit on the front pew, nod, and smile. I'd imagine a different me. But in my heart of hearts, I didn't want a different me; I wanted a *me* who was aware of His great faithfulness and who saw new mercies from His hand every single morning. I wanted to be revived in Jesus and all He was and all He had done.

I longed for the fresh living water of His Spirit to pour into what had become a murky and stagnant vessel, until what overflowed was truly crystal clear and clean. Although that's what I wanted, I couldn't seem to make it happen.

I remember sitting through the conference in the middle of the auditorium, listening to the teaching and feeling lower by the session. Toward the end of the meeting, those who needed prayer were invited to go down to the front to be prayed for by one of the many speakers. I approached the front, and a woman whose passion and love had impressed me, laid her hands on my head and prayed, "I break the spirit of unbelief off this woman." When she prayed that (I'm just telling it as it happened), it felt like something in my heart physically cracked, and the heaviness immediately lifted. Joy replaced the dreary dead feeling I had almost accepted as mine.

In the days following, I opened my Bible like a new Christian, like one who had known and believed the love of God for the first time. I thought about the conference speaker's prayer. Could unbelief have taken root in my life, dried me up, and hardened my heart?

Hebrews 3:12-13 says: "Beware, brethren, lest there be in any of you an evil heart of unbelief in departing from the living God; but exhort one another daily, while it is called 'Today,' lest any of you be hardened through the deceitfulness of sin." The writer of Hebrews was speaking to brethren, to Christians, to people like me, warning believers of unbelief and telling them to encourage each other on a consistent basis, or they could be hardened by the lies of sin and even depart from the living God.

I was frightened by how close I had come to departing and asked myself how I had ever gotten to that place. Then I realized that over time, I had allowed things that had happened to plant small seeds of disappointment in my heart; these seeds had grown and hardened into unbelief. An unbelieving heart affects everything about us because we no longer expect God to intervene in our daily lives or hope to see His promises fulfilled. And even though we remain religious, we are simply on our own!

My outlook on life and even my doctrine had changed from being rooted in God's Word and the work of Christ to being rooted in experiences and disappointments. *The Living Bible* says it like this: "Beware then of your own hearts, dear brothers, lest you find that they, too, are evil and unbelieving and are leading you away from the living God."

Most of us don't lose our faith overnight; it's a slow process, especially for those who have loved Jesus sincerely for a long time. Our faith gets nibbled at by unanswered prayer, by the difficulties of life, and by things that don't turn out the way we thought they should. If we don't encourage ourselves daily, we can end up with a handful of crumbs, unbelieving and pessimistic. We are never expectant, never hopeful, never counting on God anymore—the light grows dim and the sparkle disappears.

A definition of hope I heard years ago and have often heard repeated since then stuck with me: "Hope is the joyful expectation of the goodness of God." When we no longer expect to be touched by His gentle hand, then we have lost hope, and without it, it is hard for faith to survive. Faith and hope go hand in hand; one needs the other. "And now these three remain: faith, hope and love" (I Cor. 13:13).

We can tell we have given up hope when we no longer pray for a situation in which we believed God was going to intervene.

The prayer we lifted to the God of the impossible has turned into a sigh of resignation. Oh, well.

It doesn't take too many of those "Oh, well" sighs to replace a life of steady trust in a God who is personal and present with a distant nod to "someone out there": someone who could but won't, someone whom we used to know and depend on, but whose existence we now merely acknowledge.

"Encourage each other while it is today." (Hebrews 3:13) Lift each other up with the message of the Good News that transcends every apparent letdown. Remember the times He touched your life in practical and precious ways, otherwise, what didn't happen grows and dwarfs the times when God came through.

So, it was back to the basics for me, back to the message of the Cross, back to the love of God manifested in His Son and all He did. That's what refreshed my soul and broke the hardness; back to the book that feeds and nourishes. Back to Jesus, more of Him and less of me and my effort.

Just a few days after the speaker prayed for me at the conference and my faith had been revived, I had the dream again. The train was leaving, so I started to sprint. I was going to miss it, so I ran harder, and just as it was pulling out, I lunged for the door, was able to grab the handle, and pull myself in. I made it! I made it! I was on the train and moving forward.

For a long time, I wasn't sure what, if anything, catching the train in my subconscious mind had to do with the revival and refreshing of my faith at the leadership conference. But it had to be connected somehow because shortly after that experience, instead of missing the train, as usual, I caught it for the first time. It couldn't have been a coincidence.

Fast forward a few years to a conversation with a friend who had an odd dream and looked up its meaning on the internet. The explanation she got made sense to her, so I decided to do the same with the dream I used to have. And for what it's worth, it pointed out that if you always miss the train, it's because you feel like you almost reach your goal, but then you don't. I recognized I had never been satisfied with my spirituality back then. I often doubted what I was doing, never did enough, or did it right. I was always out of breath, standing on the platform, watching things move forward without me.

That sense of missing the mark not only makes you hard on yourself but also on others. You are aware of your shortcomings and very aware of everyone else's. You might be able to control your tongue and not point out their deficiencies, but you measure and grade them in your mind and keep an up-to-date chart of everyone's progress or lack thereof. This kind of dissatisfaction creates double frustration. Now you aren't only discontented with yourself, but become disheartened by everybody and everything.

You and everyone you know are left standing in the terminal, staring at a closed gate as the plane takes off to the land of idealism and perfection. Even God is left standing there. He, too, has fallen short on your scale of how He should be. No wonder life has lost its joy.

I'm not saying we should resign ourselves to whatever comes our way. There are times to fight, to rise up, and to push through, but we do need to come to the place where we can relax in what God has done for us through Jesus Christ. We have to differentiate between the slogans we have heard all our lives and truth.

We cannot "do whatever we set our minds to" as our mothers used to say. I have to admit that I also flung this saying around at my kids for a while, until I recognized how ridiculous it was. Another slogan I saw recently was, "The only limitation is in your mind," which is also a lie. Sometimes the limitation is in your body, your IQ, or your financial situation. Hours of ballet won't make most of us prima ballerinas, nor will art classes make us masters. There are few Olympic athletes in this world, no matter how many tried to imagine themselves on the podium with a gold medal around their necks. "Imagine it, so it will be" proved false.

There are things we will never be able to accomplish no matter how high our power of concentration or how many hours of hard work we put in. If you believe you are the only reason you haven't made it, you will continue running out of breath, missing the train, and living a life of "things should be much better than this."

We must recognize that He is the one who has placed the dreams in our hearts, and He is the one who enables us to be all He has called us to be. The plans and purposes He has for our lives will be fulfilled when we put our trust in Him and thus stop running. We can leisurely walk down the terminal to our gate and board, knowing He will get us there. We rest in the fact that the One who started the work in us is the One who will finish it. Jesus started us on our journey. He rescued us, put our feet on the path He has for us, and He will accompany us to our final destination.

CHAPTER 9

Left by the Side of the Road

No one wakes up in the morning hoping to end up stranded on the highway with the gas gauge on empty. But if it happens, the inconvenience of the moment pales in comparison to the feeling of stupidity. If there's one situation that is avoidable, it's this one.

My friend Maritza had just finished an exhausting project, and a well-deserved break was in order. I suggested we take my new car on the road, and drive into the wine country to a spa hotel.

We left Sunday after church, and the afternoon was looking perfect. I was in a new car with a favorite friend, on my way to a pleasant place. We enjoyed chatter, music, and figuring out the new media screen on the dashboard. Many miles down the road in the hills of old Castille, my friend said to me, "You seem so low in that seat. Are you sure you don't need to be higher?" I realized that she was right, so I felt around for the unused lever and raised the seat.

When I did, I saw what had been obstructed from my view by the steering wheel—the little yellow light indicating I was low on gas. Since we were going through a small town, I pulled over and asked for the station. "It's Sunday," the men at the sidewalk café said, "the station is closed." *No problem*, I thought, *there are little towns every few kilometers*. We stopped at the next one, but it was also closed. And so it went until we slid into the hotel parking lot riding on fumes.

The little gas icon had gone from a yellow warning light to flashing red, and I was grateful when we made it to our destination. I was glad what had started out as a fun trip for my friend hadn't ended up with both of us trudging down an asphalt shoulder or sitting under a tree in the middle of nowhere waiting to be rescued because of my negligence.

When we parked, we figured there were about four kilometers' worth of gas left in the tank, and the next town was about that distance away. We'd drive over after breakfast and fill up on our way back home. *No problem*.

But it wasn't really negligence that had us running on empty; it was obstructed vision. I couldn't see, and I was distracted. My car was new, and I didn't know how it worked. These things were all part of an equation that wasn't yet complete, for shortly, I would have to add "lack of information" to the mix.

When we were checking out of the hotel the next morning, I asked where the nearest gas station was. "Oh, the nearest one is closed. Everything is shut; it's a local holiday, and nothing is open today! If you drive twenty-four kilometers to the next big town, one should be open there." A regional holiday? Twenty-four kilometers up the road? Who knew? There was no way we would make it to the larger town, so I called roadside assistance from the hotel and patiently waited in the lobby for the help that was on its way.

Although everything turned out OK and we laughed about it, I admitted to my friend that I felt stupid. I had a brand new car. I should have been aware of the gas. We took off to parts unknown; I should have been more thoughtful. But in spite of human error, we had two great inventions at our fingertips— the cell phone and roadside assistance. Between the two, the whole ordeal only lasted an hour or so before we were driving down the highway toward home.

And this is how it should be on the road of life (sounds corny, I know). Even if the metaphor of a journey has been overused, we *are* driving through life on our way somewhere. Our cars aren't the only things that run out of fuel; we do. We have to watch it, or we will end up sitting on the side of the highway and not at our final destination.

I want to reach the end of my days (whether it be tomorrow or in a few decades), loving God and people, and loving them with joy. My goal is never to lose the expectancy of God's goodness in daily life, to run the race with my eyes on the One I love, excited to see Him *face-to-face* when this pilgrimage is over.

Several years ago, a young pastor spent a few days at my house. One morning while sitting in my living room, drinking coffee and talking, he asked, "How do you do it? How do you still have joy and expectancy after so many years in ministry?"

Although the roads, the scenery, and the reasons for running out vary, the means to filling up and remaining full are quite simple and always the same. We need to be aware of our gas gauge, and when we see the needle edging toward *E*, we have to recharge and refuel. We fill up, but before we know it, we are empty again. Could we be going about this the wrong way?

Perhaps we expected a well-deserved break to do more for us than it was capable of doing. Although disconnecting and relaxing a few days at the beach do me as much good as the next person, it isn't able to keep me going for very long. A few days later, the beach is a distant memory, and daily life is as draining as ever. What I hoped would put the spring back in my step or return the sparkle to my eyes proved temporary at best.

How did Jesus deal with the tiredness of his busy life? He was endlessly pulled in all directions by throngs of needy people. Yet He gave Himself willingly to one and all. John gives us a detailed account of Jesus resting at Jacob's Well. Wearied from the journey, He sent the disciples into town to get something for them to eat. But when they came back a little while later with food, He let them know that His nourishment had come from another source.

This account of Jesus taking a break is part of a well-known story about His encounter with a Samaritan woman. I love this story. Jesus was tired, but the woman was empty. She only came to the well at midday when the sun was high and the temperature hot so she could avoid the other women who came to draw water in the cool of the day. They all knew her past, and she'd rather not see them. Being looked down on and talked about is not a nice feeling. It's bad enough to feel like a failure, but insult is added to injury when people around you are repelled by your mistakes, cast you sideward glances, whisper behind your back, and give you a wide berth.

I try to imagine the Samaritan woman when she was young. She probably had the same dreams most young women have. I've never met a girl yet who has said to me, "I'd like to have about four or five failed marriages...yeah, five heartbreaks sounds about right." No, no one starts out in life hoping to be hurt or hurt others. Most just respond to life as it happens, using the tools that they've picked up through previous experiences. Those tools aren't usually helpful.

Why she had five husbands, no one knows. Chances are that if five guys left, either she was a handful or she "really knew how to pick 'em." Excuse me for judging here, but apparently, something was not working out.

In spite of her history, you do have to admire the woman. She tried to love five times. Imagine saying, "I do" *five different times,* and believing each one would be "till death do us part." How brave of her, considering that most people throw in the towel after a couple of failed marriages.

Imagine how many people she must have known. With each husband, came his large, extended, Mediterranean family, which included in-laws, their relatives, and friends. How tongues must have wagged after each failed marriage and how her heart must have hurt with each bit of gossip she heard. Everyone in town must have known all about her, so it's no wonder she went to the well after everyone else had already been there.

What would it feel like to be that woman in a small town today, where everyone had been to one of your weddings or was related to an ex-husband in one way or another? You might encounter fake smiles, superficial hellos, or complete rejection by those with whom you had once been close. If you had to make a trip to the grocery store, you would probably go around two in the morning just to protect yourself from stares, comments, and awkward moments.

Now let's see the irony of this encounter: the woman who was trying to hide from everyone who might know something about her ended up talking to a man who knew *everything* about her. When He saw her coming down the path to the well, He knew her and loved her immediately. He was aware that water wasn't what she needed that day. She needed Him and the living water that He freely offered. He knew she would finally be satisfied.

Five husbands—Jesus knew all about every one of them. We aren't given the details, but Jesus knew the reason behind every failure. Isn't that amazing? He knew all about them. He knows all about us, yet He loves us. I've sometimes found myself approaching God in prayer as if I'm going to let Him in on a secret about myself that He isn't aware of, expecting to hear a heavenly gasp of shock or a sigh of disappointment. But Jesus is no more surprised by my shortcomings, failures, and sins than He was by the Samaritan woman's. He sees the longing of every heart and desires to quench the thirst with something that satisfies forever.

As she walked toward the well, she surely noticed a stranger there, a young male stranger. Use your imagination for a minute. What was she thinking when she saw his lone figure there? Remember, she had known a lot of guys and probably didn't have a high opinion of the male gender. As she approached the well, her wall of protection must have been high, wide, and rock hard.

We read a portion of this account in John 4:7-20,25-29:

When a Samaritan woman came to draw water, Jesus said to her, "Will you give me a drink?" (His disciples had gone into the town to buy food.)

The Samaritan woman said to him, "You are a Jew and I am a Samaritan woman. How can you ask me for a drink?" (For Jews do not associate with Samaritans.)

Jesus answered her, "If you knew the gift of God and who it is that asks you for a drink, you would have asked him and he would have given you living water."

"Sir," the woman said, "you have nothing to draw with and the well is deep. Where can you get this living water? Are you greater than our father Jacob, who gave us the well and drank from it himself, as did also his sons and his livestock?

Jesus answered, "Everyone who drinks this water will be thirsty again, but whoever drinks the water I give them will never thirst. Indeed, the water I give them will become in them a spring of water welling up to eternal life."

The woman said to him, "Sir, give me this water so that I won't get thirsty and have to keep coming here to draw water."

He told her, "Go, call your husband and come back." "I have no husband," she replied.

Jesus said to her, "You are right when you say you have no husband. The fact is, you have had five husbands, and the man you now have is not your husband. What you have just said is quite true."

"Sir," the woman said, "I can see that you are a prophet. Our ancestors worshiped on this mountain, but you Jews claim that the place where we must worship is in Jerusalem." ... "I know that Messiah" (called Christ) "is coming. When he comes, he will explain everything to us."

Then Jesus declared, "I, the one speaking to you—I am he."

Just then his disciples returned and were surprised to find him talking with a woman. But no one asked, "What do you want?" or "Why are you talking with her?"

Then, leaving her water jar, the woman went back to the town and said to the people, "Come, see a man who told me everything I ever did. Could this be the Messiah?"

What would this Bible story sound like today?

Jesus: Hey, would you mind giving me a drink of water?

Woman: Why are you asking me for water? I'm a Samaritan, you're a Jew—what's your deal? What do you really want? *(Read: BACK OFF!)*

Jesus: If you knew who I was, you wouldn't be cold and distant. I don't want one single thing you have to offer. I, on the other hand, have something that you need and want. If you knew what it was, you'd ask me for it.

Woman: *(softening and beginning to let the wall down)* What are you talking about? You don't have anything to draw with, and the well is deep. You selling something?

Jesus: What I can offer you is so wonderful. It will satisfy your thirst, once and forever. It will be like a spring that just keeps bubbling up. You will never need another drink from this well or any other—ever.

Woman: Oh, wow, I'd love that! Yes, please give me some. I'd love to be satisfied and *never* have to come back to this place, ever again.

Jesus: Call your husband.

Woman: *(OUCH)* Don't have one.

Jesus: You're right about that. You've had five, and you're shacked up with a guy now.

Woman: *(Gasps!)* How do you know this!? You must be a prophet. What's your denomination? Do you believe in the same details of worship we do?

I find it interesting that as He was seeing straight into her heart and was offering her living water, she got distracted with the details of ritual. She wanted to know the particulars of His beliefs. How much easier it is to get religious than to get real!

Jesus, however, was not distracted. He let her know the time was coming when the *place* where she worshiped wouldn't be important but *how* she worshiped would be. And the Father was looking for those who worship Him in spirit and in truth. Jesus went on to tell her that *He* was the long-awaited Messiah, and she believed Him.

His words must have cut to her heart because she forgot all about her morning chores or what others might say or think of her; she ran to find the people she normally avoided and let them know about Jesus. "He knows all about me, everything I've ever done," she said.

The disciples came back about that time with lunch. They had left a tired and hungry Jesus, but when they offered Him food and encouraged Him to eat, He said that He had food they didn't know about. They were puzzled, wondering if anybody from the village had fed Him. But Jesus explained that he had been nourished by doing the will of the Father. Just seeing the woman receive salvation had filled Him up and sustained Him. I can imagine His joy as He saw the woman leave her pot and take off to tell the men in the town that the Messiah had come. Seeing her receive the revelation of salvation was like a hearty meal; it nourished and strengthened Him.

Although our situation is very different from this story, like Jesus, we can stay full by joyfully giving out to others. Our hearts will be nourished as we feed others, and our thirst is quenched when we offer a drink of everlasting life to those the Father brings to us.

So, perhaps the tiredness you feel won't be fixed by a weekend at the spa or disconnecting from all that wearies you. Although physical and mental rest is vital, it should be accompanied by giving out. We get renewed by giving. We get satisfied by filling others up. We rest by doing the Father's will.

Although for some people, His will includes selling all and moving to a far-off land, for most, it means sitting at the well, even in a tired and hungry state, and watching for the one the Father brings to you. You listen, you commune, and you wait.

They might walk into your business, sit next to you on the plane, wait on your table, or be a familiar face whose name you know. When your words or actions lift their burden, give them hope, or speak life to them, weariness also lifts from your soul.

When we forget that the Father has an eternal purpose for our lives and take our eyes off the one who satisfies, everyday life drains us dry. We find ourselves completely on empty, where we can't even get our motors to turn over at all, much less get going toward our destination again.

When my joy-of-doing-the-Father's-will gauge sits on empty, and it sometimes does, I raise my heart and hands to heaven, taking time to remember all He has done and where I have come from. Then, receiving again the life salvation brings, I become aware once more that the water He gives *is* living, that it is a well of water springing up in me, which satisfies my soul with an abundance spilling over to satisfy others.

CHAPTER 10

It's Not Just a Trickle

Initially, when we first begin to walk with Jesus, every day starts with a sunrise painted by our Father just for us. Every day ends with a sigh of gratitude for all He has done. His protection is personal, and His provision is counted on to meet our every need.

In the first few weeks and even the first years as new Christians, we are amazed at the changes wrought in our lives. We are surprised how God not only changes us but even uses us to bless other people. There is a sense of awe about it all: the fact that He loves us and cares about us blows us away. But then, to think that God All-Powerful is so concerned about the world He created that He will use anyone, even us, to touch people with His love, astounds us even more.

We are aware of so many newly found privileges: for the first time, we have a book in our hands that is actually alive, one that speaks to us and pierces our hearts and souls. We start every morning reading it, and it becomes a hearty breakfast for our hearts, setting us on track for the rest of the day. Every evening before bed, a chapter or two is a delicious midnight snack, which consoles us if the day has been rough and gives us hope for the coming day. We find ourselves going to sleep with a sweet taste in our mouths.

Besides the written Word, we discover the privilege of hearing God's voice via His Spirit speaking to our hearts. The first time we feel His guidance, we are filled with wonder once more that God—*God*—wants to communicate with *us*, lead us, help us out, and stay with us. We had no idea He was so personal or that we could be aware of the omnipresent One.

My friend, Scott, who had just recently given his life to the Lord, told me a story I will always remember. He was lonely and wished he had friends to hang out with. He felt the Lord say to his heart, "I'll be your friend."

Although he found it hard to believe, he answered back with some hesitation, "Then, let's go shopping, friend." And off he went, wondering if he was truly being accompanied by the Lord or if he had just imagined that voice or maybe even made it up. Still, it seemed real, so he decided to buy some shirts he needed. He was looking through the rack and saw one he liked. Holding it up and admiring the front, he said out loud, "I like this one. What do you think?"

Immediately, he heard an inward voice say, "I like that one too, but there's a problem. There's a hole in the back of the shirt."

He had only seen the front of the shirt, so he knew this was a moment of truth. Was this really the Lord? If there was no hole, then he had made it all up, and this I'll-be-your-friend thing would not be true. He even wondered if maybe he was crazy and had started hearing imaginary voices. After a long time of wavering, he had to know for sure. He turned it around and looked. There it was! There *was* a hole in the back of the shirt the size of a small coin.

As a new Christian, he had never read James 2:23, where Abraham was called the friend of God, but shortly thereafter, he came across that verse. That shopping experience sealed the truth of God's friendship in his heart. When we first discover that God our Creator not only saves us but also desires to do life with us, it's humbling and makes us want to do life right.

So many things, which have worried and concerned us, are now eclipsed by things much more important. We feel privileged to be a part of what He is doing on the Earth, and instead of investing our time and lives on things that will not last, suddenly, we are a part of eternal things, and we serve Him enthusiastically. Any opportunity to share the Word, help, or bless someone seems good to us. "I'll go wherever you want; I'll do whatever you say, I'll sleep or not sleep, eat or not eat—just use my life for Your glory, Lord." And with that prayer on our lips, we tackle life with gusto.

Way back when, before the seatbelt law, my former husband owned a Ford pickup truck. Four thin people could fit in the front seat, not comfortably, but if squeezed tight, the door could shut. Many a weekend, we would pick up another young couple and then drive for many hours to Baja California to help with a new church plant there. Although it wasn't a real big deal or even a true sacrifice, to us, it had the smell of eternity, and we did it with great joy and honor. There was a happy feeling in the pickup as we bumped along the road to Baja and back. We had the sense of purpose and wonder that believers always have when they realize they are part of something that will last forever.

But for some reason, as the months turn into years, we lose the wonder of it all—the wonder of the message and the wonder of the walk. Some people lose it sooner than others, but for most, it takes a while. By the time the pages of our first Bible begin to ruffle and the back of the binding breaks, many have already become so ho-hum about redemption's story that what was once so precious is now an obligation, a duty, and a religious performance. We weigh the time and trouble of any ministry to see what it's worth to us, and seldom ever stop long enough to listen to His voice.

I've thought a lot about the reasons for this. Why does it happen? The message has not changed. Even years after conversion, we still know we were bound for hell, without hope and devoid of purpose, but what has happened to the sparkle once in our eyes when we talk about Him now? Where, when, and why does it move from the supernatural awareness of being among the privileged few to something so taken for granted it becomes boring? The savory snack from the Word every morning becomes more like eating your oatmeal, and the sense of touching God in evening prayer before our eyes close has somehow become *now I lay me down to sleep*, devoid of faith or feeling.

God has not changed; He is the same, so whatever has happened, happened to us, not Him. What has happened to us? Could it be that we just forgot from whence we came?

I was talking to a man I met at a conference in Barcelona some time ago. He was from Mexico, spoke several languages, and specialized in Muslim and Central Asian missions. He had the poise of a diplomat and the manners of a prince. Since I had grown up in Mexico City, we had a lot to talk about. He told me about the part of the city where he had grown up, and how he had been raised in extreme poverty with very little hope for a future outside of the slum, yet life and God had smiled upon him. Had he told me his parents were university professors, I would never have doubted it. There was no trace of "slum" in anything he said or did. I enjoyed hearing his stories about all he was presently doing and had recently done, but what stuck with me was this comment:

"Every time I go back to Mexico City, I go to the area where I grew up. I look at my house. I watch the little children in that slum and I remember—I remember—lest I forget and start to believe I have had anything to do with the comfortable and fulfilling life I now live. I would still be there if it were not for God's love and grace."

All of us should take a trip back to *our* slum on a regular basis. We should breathe in the former smells and the polluted air of life without Jesus, kick the garbage around in a world, which is no longer home, but still familiar. We need to keep that place alive in our memory because when we leave our little walk down memory lane and return to the place where God has brought us, where the air is unpolluted by sin and self, gratitude replaces familiarity and expectancy replaces boredom. We have been translated from the Kingdom of darkness into the Kingdom of Light, and we need never forget it.

Even in the physical world, good things become the norm after a while. Conveniences unheard of just a few years ago, we now consider our personal right. Unfortunately, the same thing happens in our spiritual lives. We forget that not everyone lives with their sins forgiven. We forget that not everyone comes home to a relatively tension-free house. We forget that not everyone lives without the tormenting fear of death and dying. All of these amazing privileges, which cost our Lord everything, begin to be commonplace, and our memory fails us. It was not always so. We did not always live this way.

Over time, the picture of what we were really like becomes blurry, and we become convinced it was our own hard work and self-determination that improved us and gave us a new start. We forget we were losers and on the road to nowhere special. If we aren't careful, we forget that it was God who pulled us out of the pit, cleaned us up, and restored us to a right relationship with Him. He put dreams in our hearts, dreams of change and purpose. We must remember. We must remind ourselves that the average Joe does not have what we have gotten so used to.

God was the one who began to heal the hurt places in our lives and mend the broken areas. As He changed us, walking in His grace became second nature. Things that once tempted us no longer had any attraction at all. Character weakness that made life hard and relationships difficult began to be strengthened, and we became more likeable and easier to live with. We had become new creations. The old was gone. The new had come.

I know entire families that were changed because one member became a Christian. As that member argued less, became more giving, was no longer so self-centered, the atmosphere in the house changed, even though no one else became a Christian. If one of the elements in the household becomes nicer, everyone in the house can breathe easier, and the atmosphere in the home becomes more livable. That's great! God transforms one person, and many are affected, but it is God's transforming work. We need to continue depending on Him every day and be aware we don't just improve or mellow with age, because we don't.

We *need* Him. We will never have this Christian living thing down. I had a feeling, way back when, that, eventually, I would be so good at Christianity that I could flip the switch to auto-pilot and glide through life's turbulent skies, away from the controls and with very few bumps. But it never happened. God's creation was made to depend on Him. We will always need Him. Every day will be a walk of faith, and that walk must lead us daily to Jesus, where we receive the freshness of all He has done for us.

When we forget that we depend on Him, it's just not fun any-more. We become the source to supply our own need for love, hope, and faith, which turns into nothing but a lot of work. Before long, the daily Christian grind allows weariness to set in—our lives become filled with boring, monotonous religion. No one wants it, yet so many of us endure it because we never even noticed that our well ran dry and has been empty for a long, long time. The spring dried up, and the ground is hard, but we go through the motions and silently wonder where the joy of our salvation has gone.

When we no longer expect God's intervention in our lives on a daily basis, there really isn't much to look forward to. For the most part, tomorrow will be like today, and the next day will be like tomorrow was, with a little beach, skiing, or Disneyworld peppered here and there.

Oh, of course, we continue to attend church faithfully and never forget to tithe, but we no longer go to God for satisfaction. Because of that, we put forth tremendous self-effort and expend our stamina in figuring it all out and keeping life going. How easily we become bored, lifeless, and dissatisfied.

Bored is a dangerous place to be in your Christian life. We might vaguely remember a happier time, but now, when we have exhausted our own sources, we ask ourselves if maybe we are dissatisfied because *someone* didn't keep *His* side of the bargain. Life was supposed to be great living for Jesus. Life was supposed to be fulfilling and, hey, wasn't I supposed to be rich by now? When we're thirsty and have forgotten where the water is, it's easy to second-guess our life choices and look for the guilty party. Unfortunately, our finger ends up pointing toward heaven more often than not. "I trusted Him," someone once told me through clenched teeth, "and *He* let me down."

Perhaps we have been misinformed and ill-taught about what a blessed and fruitful life really is. Our lives have been infiltrated by the lies and deceptions of the world outside. Society insinuates that abundant life is something you can put in your bank account or drive out your driveway, and many books and sermons back it up.

But the abundant life is something deep within us, it's the living water that wells up into eternal life. This water, this life, cannot be bought or sold, painted or renovated, rocked in a nursery or even walked down the aisle. Abundant life is something so real that nothing and no one can take it from us. If abundant life is made up of houses and lands or family and friends, then the abundant life can disappear. What kind of life did the Savior purchase on the Cross for us if that is the case? Is the life He gives so material that it can be downgraded, worn out, repossessed, or die? No, of course not!

We can't be new Christians our entire lives, but we don't have to lose the joy of living for Jesus. The thief comes to kill our joy, steal our expectancy, and destroy our faith, and he does it when we forget where life comes from and who it is that supplies it.

Jesus came that we might have *life* and lots of it. He didn't come so that abundant life would trickle down to us, but so living water would flow to us and then from us. In John 7:37, Jesus stood up and shouted out an invitation to all who were within His hearing, "If anyone is thirsty, let him come to me and drink."

He continues to shout it to us. He doesn't whisper the offer. He raises his voice because He is seriously offering us the only thing that can help us. He is offering us *Himself*. "Come to me and drink; come to me and drink." When we hear Him, we should respond by running to Him daily and drinking deeply. When we do, our faith will remain fresh, and His Word becomes even tastier over time. His voice will be sweet, and the message of His love will always fill us with wonder.

CHAPTER 11

Seasons

The new circumstance looked dreary. I was twenty-three years old and driving to a place I had never been before. We were going there to stay, at least for a while and maybe forever, so I was disappointed to see it was a lot deader, flatter, and drier than the pictures I had seen or the articles I had read about it. There were a few hills on the horizon and what some might call mountains way out there, but for the most part, it was barren. The dirt was red and rocky—fields of rock.

Nothing was green; even the olive trees were short and silvery gray, not trees really. I was unenthused about the place we had landed, but had no choice but to get busy adjusting. We needed to find a permanent place to stay, figure out what to do, and how to share the love of Jesus with people who seemed very different from us.

There was a hill just outside of town where we walked in the afternoons. We bundled up, took a stroll, and looked out onto the nothingness. It was bleak. Then, after a few weeks, the weather warmed, and the view wasn't so brown anymore. This city girl had no idea what winter wheat was, but it started coming up and covering the formerly barren fields. The rocks disappeared, and the red earth turned to a brilliant green. It was bright and beautiful.

In what seemed like just a few days, green was everywhere. The wheat even grew around the olive trees, making it look like they were standing on a bright shag carpet. Shortly after the sprigs of grain came up, red poppies appeared. They weren't sparsely sprinkled, but looked like an artist had dipped the brush in vermillion red and generously covered the canvas. Abundant almond trees burst into white blossoms like brides walking down the path on the way to their weddings. It took my breath away. How had that rocky, barren terrain turned into something so beautiful? Soon after, our hill was further sprinkled with flowering thyme, rosemary, and wild lavender.

Who knew? I had no idea what I had judged useless and ugly could become so beautiful.

I knew nothing about the seasons in the new place I lived. In fact, I knew little about seasons anywhere. I grew up in a semi-tropical climate where the sun usually shone, and a thick sweater was what constituted a winter wrap. Had I known that change was coming, I wouldn't have complained or judged but could have waited it out patiently and with anticipation.

After that first year and every year after that, I eagerly awaited spring, knowing that beauty and warmth were just pages away on my calendar. I got excited over the first poppies by the side of the road and the wild lavender in the hills. I must mention that storks fly up from Africa to nest on church belfries and cast a watchful eye on what goes on down below in the town squares.

And if someone local takes time to teach you, you can pick wild asparagus. At first, you can't make them out among the brush, but with practice, you can get a nice bunch to fry up in olive oil.

Unfortunately, in the circumstances of our own lives, we don't know when or if winter will turn to spring. If we knew, the rocky fields would soon be beautiful, and we could endure the present barrenness with expectation and joy. A teacher of mine once said you could stand anything as long as you knew it wasn't permanent, and that's true. It's the open-ended story that fills us with anxiety and dread. What if nothing ever changes? What am I going to do then?

A young friend called from overseas a few years ago to talk to me. She was distressed, not only because she was hitting thirty and was still unmarried, but she hadn't had a date in months. She began to weep over the phone, and I tried to console her with, "Sally," (not her real name) "I would love to tell you that your husband is just around the corner and that God has someone for you, but I can't tell you that. I do have a question for you. What if Mr. Right never comes along? What *if* you never get married or have another date, are you going to cry your way through life like you are crying now?" She sniffled a bit, and we talked about the seasons of life and what it means to trust God when you aren't sure if things are ever going to turn out the way you had imagined.

No one wants to stay in a hard place forever. All of us want change for the better in every season of our lives, to move out of winter into spring, but hating where we are only makes everything gloomier.

I've always been averse to slogans that simplify the complicated. When someone tosses a little ditty out there to the frustrated heart, it seldom benefits them. Phrases like "if life gives you lemons, make lemonade" are often thrown around by people who were handed the lemonade on a silver tray, ice cubes included, and it makes you want to slug 'em. Yet there is a seed of truth in all of those seemingly silly sayings. We all know people who didn't even get lemons to start with, and yet yielded their lives to the Lord and allowed Him to make something sweet and thirst-quenching, despite the circumstances.

Those first few weeks in Spain, I wondered if God knew what He was doing. It all came out of a lack of trust that God is indeed a good God. All of us go through times when we wonder if He is looking out for us in a personal way. We say we believe, and we want to, but when it comes right down to it, we don't think God is doing an excellent job of taking care of things, or we wouldn't have ended up where we are. We look out on the barren rocky fields of our present and don't like it much. If our today is bleak, what is the guarantee that our future will bloom into anything different?

Jesus had a good bit to say about wishing our circumstances and unchangeable situations were different. There are so many things that we'd like to alter, yet He said that we can't add an hour to our lives, even if we long for it. And how many more things that aren't as important as length of days do we wish for? "Wish I were taller, taller, taller." "Wish I lived some-where else, somewhere else, somewhere else." "Wish I may, wish I might have the wish I wish tonight." *But wishing it never makes it happen; it only makes dissatisfaction with the present worse.* The good news is that Jesus helps us out by showing us the root of our worry. If we understand why we do what we do, then we can deal with the cause instead of the symptom.

Sometimes I put this passage in my own words to understand it better. This is the way I read Matthew 6:25-30 to myself: "I'm telling you. Don't obsess over your life, what you're going to eat, or drink or about what clothes you wish were hanging in your closet. Isn't life about more than food and clothes? Look up to the sky and see the birds flying around; they don't seem to be starving, nor do they seem to be striving about where their next meal will come from. Why not? Because *your* Heavenly Father feeds them. Surely you are more important to

Him than they are. And who can live a longer life by imagining it? Why do you spend so much time thinking about having the right things to wear? Look at the wildflowers in the fields. They don't go shopping, but they are better dressed than royalty. Now, if God dresses the weeds in colorful flowers that disappear overnight, won't He be sure you look OK, Rebecca, of little faith?"

He nails it, as usual. He doesn't mince words and goes straight to the point; you worry because you don't trust your heavenly Father. You lack faith in His love and goodness. You think He cares more about the birds than He cares about you and that His concern is for fields and flowers.

A woman came up to me for prayer after a meeting once. She told me that she was beset by worry that often turned to tormenting fear. I asked her, "What are you afraid of?" She looked at me and said, "Everything. Everything. Everything." I could tell that she was paralyzed by apprehension in every area, and it made me sad for her. Waiting for the other shoe to drop all the time is no way to live; neither is looking out the window to curse the winter when the only one who can change the season is our heavenly Father.

Oh, for joy and trust in the seasons of life. We long for a baby. Then we can't wait for him to be out of diapers; we're ready for him to start school. Oh, no! Where did the time go? We don't want him to graduate! We don't want him to move out.

We long to have the baby back. The baby moves back in. Now we want an empty nest as our friends have. We want to travel. We can't now; we're helping raise grandkids.

Oh, the rocky fields of life! When will things change; when will spring come? Where is that dream job? Where is that dreamboat? When will the tide turn? When will I be truly satisfied?

Satisfaction in the future hinges on our satisfaction now. When I think back on my first weeks of looking out over the rocky fields, I wish I could have found beauty in the colors of ochre and sienna, in the shadows and open vistas. It would have made the change even more beautiful. Spring wouldn't have come as a relief from a situation, but as a progression of learning and life. "Bloom where you are planted" is another phrase that bugs me because, again, it often comes out of the mouth of someone living in Beverly Hills, but it can happen. You *can* be planted and produce a bouquet *anywhere*.

My Aunt Nell moved from living in her own house to assisted living in a different state near my cousin Sherrie. She had lived most of her life in the same city and was well known for years of teaching kindergarten, Sunday school, and summer camps. She is known for her strength, contentment, and giving. On her birthday, she receives up to a hundred calls wishing her a blessed year because her kindness has touched so many.

I wondered how she was going to make a move from a place she had lived for over seventy years independently, surrounded by people of all ages, to living under one roof with dozens of elderly people in a new state.

I called her to see how she was doing. "Aunt Nell, how are you? Do you like it? Are you happy?" Her response was classic Nell, and it will be with me forever.

"Oh, sugar, I liked it before I saw it and I was happy before I got here."

In other words, *"Where* I am has nothing to do with *how* I am."

It would be great to live that way: content, happy, expecting good things, peaceful in the plans of the One who loves us more than we know. When I think of resting and not stressing, my mind often goes to a hammock on a beach. In my imagination, I'm lying there, the sun is warm, a gentle breeze is blowing the palm trees, and the waves are lulling me to sleep; I haven't a care in the world. That is how we would love our hearts and minds to be all the time, but we slip back into dissatisfaction over things that we have no power to improve, much less alter permanently. We often live with a sense of foreboding and concern and make Murphy's Law our statement of faith.

It is possible to live in the stillness of the assurance that trust brings, or Jesus wouldn't have encouraged us to rest there. There's no comparison between a beach hammock and His everlasting arms, nor between a sea breeze and the whispering of His promises in our ear, promises that He is in charge and that He is good.

CHAPTER 12

It's Hot in Here

W e don't really know what our house of faith is made of until the unexpected waves of disappointment and hardship relentlessly crash up against it. When they do, we find out quickly if the faith we proclaimed was simply theory or if it was reality.

From the moment we first come to Christ, we begin building our life of faith. This is a timely construction process. At first, it seems to go up quickly as we lay brick upon brick of experience, devotion, and dedication, trusting we are cementing it with sound theology. The structure appears sturdy and looks great. We want to believe we are building an enduring structure that will stand the test of time and keep us safe until the day we don't need it anymore, the day we will be moving for good, away from this fragile life to the eternal one.

Week after week, year in and year out, I had told the people who came to me with any kind of problem that in Christ they had all they needed. I told many a man, many a woman, and many a friend that Christ was all sufficient. Even though their circumstances were less than perfect, He was more than enough, not only to help them, but when invited *all the way* into their lives, Jesus Christ would be all He has promised— Healer, Restorer, and Friend.

He could restore the broken places of their hearts and emotions and even fill the empty spaces in their homes and lives. He could and He would if only given the chance. After all, wasn't the God of the universe large enough to fill the cracks and crevices of a human life? Wasn't the God of love enough love? Wasn't His presence superior to any human company? I encouraged people to look beyond their everyday emptiness to the God of the heavens, who filled everything, and to believe He would fill them and fulfill them. Then, I would leave them and return home to a husband, to children, and to a life packed with people, activity, and affirmation, to a place where my preaching had not yet been tested.

But things changed when I began to feel tremors in what I had thought was unmovable, solid ground. I tried to ignore them, thinking it was just a passing phase, but the tremors got stronger, and it slowly dawned on me that my husband just might leave me.

I should point out we were a couple that never said the "D" word. We taught marriage seminars. We were thought of as the happy couple, and many people wished they had a marriage like ours. So, when I say it slowly dawned on me, it was because my seismograph had never detected more than a light tremor, and the thought of a major fault running down the middle of our lives was inconceivable, a broken home unimaginable. Besides the death of a child, life without my husband was the worst thing I could think of happening, and with the shocking realization that maybe, just maybe, he would leave, came wave upon wave of paralyzing fear.

I had just left a counseling session and was in the car with my friend Rena, who knew what was going on. I was sad. I was distraught. "Rebecca," she said, "What is the worst thing that could happen?" I couldn't even look at her. I couldn't get the word out. She repeated her question several times, "What is the worst thing that could happen?"

I finally blurted it out, "He could leave; he could divorce me."

She touched my hand and said, "Yes, he could, and if he does, God is big enough."

"God is *big* enough to see you through." That is what I had taught, that is what I had believed. And in that car with my friend, even though I felt like I was sinking into painful darkness and that life was crumbling around me, *I knew,* without a shadow of a doubt, that it was true. God was big enough. God had always been big enough, and He would be big enough now.

I ask that question to others now when they are frightened of the future. "What is the worst thing that could happen?" Vocalize it. Say it. And then remember and confess that *even* if the worst happens, God is big enough. He is there in the midst of it all, but you must acknowledge His presence to take full advantage of the help He generously offers and recognize that no circumstance can separate you from Him.

I remember the hardest, saddest, and most terrifying day when I knew for sure my husband was going to leave. A verse in Romans sprang up in my heart: "Nor things present, nor things to come...nor things present, nor things to come..." The words surged up inside of me, and I was buoyed for days. God had not left. He was sticking with me through thick and thin. "For I am convinced that neither death nor life, neither angels nor demons, neither the present nor the future, nor any powers, neither height nor depth, nor anything else in all creation, will be able to separate us from the love of God that is in Christ Jesus our Lord." (Romans 8:38,39)

What can separate us from the love of God? Not things *present*, nor things to come. The things, which at the moment are unbearably painful and seem impossible to survive can't separate us from *Him*. He *is present* in the present. He *is there* and longs to reveal to us how big He really is. He is enough for us.

When we recognize Him and receive Him into the situations of our lives, nothing can destroy us. On our own, we're toast.

But with Him, we can bear anything and come out on the other side with our faith intact—amazingly, even our joy will survive.

He is present. He is Emmanuel, God with us. We must remember this when the sky darkens and the rain of sorrow pelts down on us. We might think we are sinking in its flood but He is with us, just like He was with the disciples long ago in the boat as they crossed the lake of Galilee and were surprised by severe weather. It's the unexpected that can toss us about, cause us to lose our grip, and throw us overboard. Just like the disciples, we do what we can and we do what we know. And when we've done it, we do it over again. When we realize that, in spite of our master boatman skills, we are out of control, like them, we panic.

The fishermen disciples had gotten to shore safely with their know-how many a time, but not this time. This storm was too big, too fierce, too frightening, beyond even their experience, so the sailors woke the carpenter up, and He calmed their storm. They didn't expect Him to do anything miraculous; it wasn't His area of expertise. They were just bothered that He was sleeping and not participating in the terror of the moment with them. At least panic with us, for heaven's sake, Master!

Had they understood that God-made-flesh was in the boat with them and not merely a teacher-carpenter, they could have joined Him for a nap, as they were tossed about, and ridden out the storm snoozing. God would never sink to the bottom of the lake and drown, and God-made-flesh was with them. He was present, just as He is present with us in the unexpected squalls of life. We need not wait until we have used every resource and are emotionally exhausted before we call to Him, "Don't you care?" Of course, He does.

The three Hebrew children, whose story is told in Daniel, had an amazing revelation about God, who was "a very present help in times of trouble" (Psalm 46:1). Their faith in Him was unwavering. When faced with a decision of either bowing and worshiping a golden image made by King Nebuchadnezzar or standing tall and honoring the living God, they chose to stand, even if it meant certain death. They proclaimed God would deliver them out of the fire, but they put a disclaimer on their declaration: even if He didn't, they weren't about to go back on what they knew to be true about Him. Only He deserved their obedience and worship. He was the living God. The image of gold was tall and imposing, but dead and lifeless. There was no doubt about who deserved their devotion.

We know the story. They refused to pay homage to the king's image, so they were tied up and tossed into the fire. But instead of turning to charcoal, they stood up and started walking around in the furnace. King Nebuchadnezzar looked in and not only saw them on their feet doing just fine, but also saw someone else present with them. I like how the passage reads in the *King James Version*, "Lo, I see four men loose, walking in the midst of the fire, and they have no hurt; and the form of the fourth is like the Son of God" (Daniel 3:25). His form was like the Son of God because He *was* the Son of God. He was there. He had arrived and the fire was still hot. But it didn't hurt them; it only burned away the ropes tying them up.

This same thing can happen to us. We can be thrown into circumstances that would normally kill a person's spirit and burn up a person's hope. And instead of being consumed, we come out on the other side a freer person. Although the Hebrew children were thrown in bound up, the ropes were burned off of them. Yet, when they came out, they didn't even smell of smoke. That is amazing. That is an incredible promise to anyone who experiences the fire and feels the heat. No matter what happens, we don't have to walk around scorched the rest of our lives. When He walks with us, no matter what is subtracted, what changes, or what we lose, we don't have to carry that campfire smell.

When I was a young wife, Paula, a counselor friend of mine, told me that when she was in a room of women, she could immediately tell who was divorced. "Really?" I asked, "How is that?" She could see rejection in their eyes, she said. For some reason, that statement stuck with me for years. And now that I was headed for divorce, I didn't want to be the woman in the room with the "rejected eyes" or carry around the "yep, she got dumped" aura. That would be like coming out of the fire whole, but with the smell of smoke lingering on my life. With Jesus walking in the fire with me, it wouldn't have to be that way. I wouldn't have to be a sad-eyed person for the rest of my life. By His grace, I would not smell of smoke.

Good things can happen in the fire, in spite of the heat and the pain. I hadn't been aware of the things that bound me; they had become so much a part of who I was that I didn't even know they were there. There were all kinds of things that mattered to me and hindered me from walking in the total freedom purchased by Jesus for me. Looking back, I realized I was smug, self-righteous, spiritually obnoxious, and an expert at judgmental zingers. I could size up someone's spirituality, dedication, or ministry in two seconds flat, and give them my silent seal of approval or disapproval, depending on the case, and finish up with an affirming nod to my own perfect record.

But in the fire—in the fire, your unrecognized bondages are exposed to the burning heat of your circumstances. And if Jesus walks with you, His truth and His presence untie and strip away sin and chains. If you open yourself up to His healing touch and gentle voice, when you step out of the fire, not only are you on your feet, but the sign of what you've been through is the lightness in your heart and the spring in your step. We can go in bound and walk out free. That is good news.

Many do lip service to God's all-sufficiency, yet don't believe He is enough to bring one out intact. Some of the same people who told me God would help me were the ones who seemed concerned that I was doing as well as I was. Even though some days I felt like I wasn't going to make it, I was *standing* in the midst of the furnace, and it just didn't seem normal to them. They were afraid I was faking it or trying to be too strong, and that I would crash when I least expected it. One even said, "I'm expecting you to crumble any day now; you have been strong too long." But, I wasn't strong; I just wasn't alone in the fire.

The first couple of years my husband was gone, I caught people looking at me with concern.

"How are you?" they would ask carefully, trying not to butt in where not invited, but concerned all the same.

"I am doing well, considering all that has happened."

"You seem to be doing too well," some would say. "Be sure you grieve, now."

When I told them not to worry because I often cried myself to sleep at night, they seemed relieved.

Some people are confused to see someone who has gone through deep pain do well. They want to see a few scars, at least, or obviously healed gashes. And when they don't, they assume it must not have hurt very much, when, in fact, the opposite is true. It hurts so very much, the fire gets so red hot, that you know this—unless you give it all to Him and invite Him into the furnace with you, you *will not* survive. For it is there, in the fire, that pain and sorrow pale in comparison to His greatness, His care, and His presence.

CHAPTER 13

Redemption

was driving with one of my dearest friends, chattering about one thing and then another when our conversation turned to the things of the Lord, and deepened.

"Do you think every situation is redemptive? Every situation?" my friend asked. At that moment, it was hard to imagine that anything good could be harvested from one that she had just described to me.

It seems impossible for something horrible to be turned into something lovely or something broken reconstructed into something that could be useful, especially when left in a state that's final. If it's broken, it's broken. If it's lost, it's lost. If it's dead, it's dead. Done. Gone. Finished.

And because it is a permanent situation and nothing can change, we are told that we should "get a grip," "man up," "keep breathing and allow time and distance to blur the details and lessen the pain." And that is what we try to do because it is impossible to imagine some situations becoming bearable, much less producing anything good. We try to put them behind us and survive.

But as Christians, we believe that there is a seed of redemption in everything that happens and that new life can come from the darkest and deadest of circumstances. At least that's what we want to believe. Romans 8:28 is preached from every pulpit, framed and hung on walls, and stuck on refrigerator magnets, "All things work together for good."

All things.

The *all* is the hard part. If it said "some things work together for good," we could agree. We can usually recognize that God is generally in our favor, and we can see an overall goodness out there, but all things seem impossible to turn around for good. There are things too destructive, too painful, and too dark.

Most people resign themselves to trying to keep the hurt manageable but never expect to be OK again, much less believe the case itself could be redemptive and bring anything positive into their lives and the lives of those around them. Sometimes things are so ugly that we would rather just keep them buried deep in the dark earth of our memory, ignored and never visited again.

Unfortunately, things that have left deep gashes in our hearts, although buried deep down, don't stay under or even remain the same size. Sooner or later, they resurface and spread. They spread to other parts of our thinking; they turn into fears and nightmares. The further you try to push the memories into the dark, the more they seem to make their appearance in the most unexpected places and at the most inconvenient times.

The feelings and thoughts that you hoped were forgotten come clawing at your mind again, trying to pick the lock that you double bolted and force their way in. Anything can bring them back; a sound, a scent, a song, an endless number of things open the floodgates of memories and feelings years after the fact. Sometimes these memories are fleeting, but other times, they turn into unreasonable reactions and responses that block the restoration and healing of our souls.

If we can't forget the event or make it disappear, what can we do with what happened? If we have talked about it, stuffed it, and prayed for it to go away and it hasn't, what else is there to do? We must do more than plead for relief; we must turn our eyes upward and invite God into the hard and awful experience and ask Him to do something supernatural, and that is to work "all things" for good in us.

Before we can do this, we have to settle something in our hearts and minds. We must believe that God is good. If we believe that God killed our child, sent the abuser our way, or is "out to get us," then there is no way we would want to welcome Him into our life. After all, He's the mean one. Why bother with one who never bothered with us in the moment of our deepest need and urgent cry?

When we are hurting because the unimaginable has happened and we feel like we are in a downward free fall spiral, an understanding of the Gospel will grab hold of us and rescue us before we hit bottom and are destroyed forever. I am no theologian and don't pretend to understand the breath of salvation or what it cost God to save us, but the bit that I do get is enough to put pain and sorrow in a scope that is larger, much larger than the day life caved in.

I had never spent a lot of time thinking about the price paid for my salvation. I was the "let's get with it," the "time's a wastin'," "work while it is still day" type, and somehow the *why* of it all got lost in the task at hand. But unless why Christ died and what He did becomes front and center in our heart, sooner or later, we will end up broken down and stranded on the side of the *God Has a Wonderful Plan For My Life Road* because the wonderful plan looks less than what the world calls wonderful a lot of the time.

Just yesterday, I spoke with a young woman who had recently lost her mother to cancer. We were talking about how hard it is when you feel like you had heard from God and that God promised and then it didn't happen. I told her that that kind of thing happened to me a lot when I was praying in faith for my marriage. Someone would encourage me to believe and then

I would get an email that said the same thing from someone else; I told her, "The rainbow would appear, the butterfly would flutter through the window, and a dew drop would fall," everything pointing to something that, in the end, did not happen.

But if I take all of those things that seem like unfulfilled promises, all that didn't go according to plan, and remember that God took my every sin, every mistake, every harsh word spoken, every manipulative act to get my way, lies (white and other colors), evil vindictive thoughts, and everything else that had me deserving hell on *Himself* to restore me to Almighty God, a restored marriage pales in comparison.

"Didn't He take my mother's cancer on the Cross?" was the question.

"Yes, He did," I said, "Jesus took your mother's cancer on His body on the Cross, so that by His stripes, she could be healed completely, and you can have her forever."

"He also took every sadness, every abuse, every evil work, every torture, every lie—things so deep and so dark that they separated Him from fellowship with His Father so that your mom would have fellowship with Him and with you *eternally*."

The message of the Gospel is familiar to many of us, yet we have never really taken a long hard look at it, welcomed it into our lives, and allowed it to touch us.

These are the facts. We were born in sin and our sin separated us from God. Even if considered a nice person by ourselves and others, we've sinned enough to deserve hell and an eternity away from God. We could not save ourselves. We needed a savior. God, our Creator, the One who spoke the world into existence became man, lived a perfect life, so that He could pay the price for our sin, so that we could receive forgiveness. "But he was wounded for our transgressions, he was bruised for our iniquities: the chastisement of our peace was upon him, and with his stripes, we are healed. All we like sheep have gone astray; we have turned everyone to his own way, and the Lord hath laid on him the iniquity of us all." (Isaiah 56:5)

My sin, your sin, her sin, his sin—everyone's sin was put on Him. Everyone's. Not only was my sin nailed to the Cross, but the sin of the ones who sinned against me was also paid for.

If one person's sin caused you suffering, it is impossible to imagine the pain Christ felt when He took it all—every evil act carried out by human beings since the beginning of time—the pain we felt multiplied by unimaginable millions on the heart of the perfect Son of God. He took the punishment so that the offenders, you and I, could be reconciled and healed.

I've tried to imagine the crushing weight of the world's sin. I can't, of course, but if I can understand the Cross just a little and see all the wrong, all the hurt, and all the despair of the entire world from the beginning of time, crushing the one man that we now call Savior, it begins to change the way I see God and change even my perspective on things that never should have happened.

Why did He let this happen or that happen? He could have stopped it! Again, I lay my unanswered questions in the scarred hands that willingly were nailed to the Cross for me.

When Jesus was standing before the Roman court, Pilate said:

"You know I have the power to kill you or set you free."

And Jesus said, "You would have no power over me if it were not given to you from above" (John 19:10,11).

He could have stopped it, but He didn't.

"No one takes it from me—*No one takes it from me*—but I lay it down of my own accord" (John 10:18).

God, our Alpha and Omega, Beginning and End, willingly gave Himself on the Cross because He knew what the outcome would be. The result of the crucifixion would be our salvation. It would crush the power of sin forever and would purchase reconciliation and eternity in His presence.

He paid it all; it cost Him everything. We don't need to appease our God with daily offerings of rice, light candles, or crawl on our knees for miles to show our sincerity and remorse. There is nothing we can add to His offering. He did it *all*. The debt of the entire world was paid in full.

When this becomes real to us, we can take a deep breath, trust, and unbolt the lock. When we crack the door to every evil memory and give Christ access into the heartbreaking experiences we have lived through, He will coax us out of the darkness with His love. We can put the pain of the death, the divorce, the rape, the abuse, the rejection in His hands and patiently watch Him do His work in areas of our lives that only His spirit can reach.

As we open the door to Him, the miracle worker invites us to step out of the sadness that we considered normal and into the glorious light of His freedom. He plants our feet on the road to redemption and wholeness and walks with us.

The very one who was good enough to bear our sorrows and carry our grief helps us relinquish the right to hate and be bitter, and our hearts begin to turn and heal. It happens on the inside—redemption is an inward thing. The past is over. It can't be altered. The evil has been done, the words have been spoken, the hurt and heartache have been caused, and nothing can be changed, but what can be changed is the damage done to our souls.

For the *joy* set before Him, He endured the Cross. If I can look at life through the lens of the Cross to the joy of knowing Him, loving Him, understanding Him a little better, I can endure.

Experiences change us forever and can make us feel like we will never be whole again, but if God's goodness is deeply rooted in our lives and if we know we are loved by the Almighty, we rest assured that He will turn all things for our good. All things.

CHAPTER 14

Risky Satisfaction

One of my co-workers, a friend from Chihuahua, Mexico, is very creative and works in a frenzy, pulling things together in an amazing, last-minute manner. She popped her head into my office late on a Thursday afternoon and asked me if I would like to go away with her to celebrate her birthday.

Her birthday was the next day; she didn't have a hotel reservation, hadn't even decided where to go, and I doubted there would be an opening since it was Valentine's Day weekend, a holiday when lots of Spanish couples get away because, in Spain, the day is not about loving everybody, from your teacher to your grandmamma, nor is it about friendship.

This day, *día de los enamorados*, the day of those in love, is about your one and only. Every "in-love" or "possibly-in-love" or "wish-they-were-in love" couple seems to take off somewhere; the restaurants and hotels are booked in advance.

So, although I thought finding a place to go would be unlikely, I told her if she found anything, I would love to celebrate her birthday with her. But I also told her not to get her hopes up. She tried anyway and did find an opening in a great place not too far away, so the next day, we drove off to celebrate her life.

We planned to swim, eat, and talk, away from the busy city and tight schedules. I woke up early the following morning in the hotel, and not wanting to disturb my friend, who was sleeping soundly, slipped out to the restaurant to read and enjoy a quiet breakfast. The restaurant was still empty. It was nice and peaceful. I got my first cup of coffee and opened my book. By the time I got my second cup, I had noticed people slowly drifting in and finding tables. I kept my coffee cup full and looked up between paragraphs to do a little people watching.

After about two hours of sips of coffee, bites of toast, and reading, something dawned on me. My table was the only table in the entire restaurant with just one person at it. I was surrounded by valentine couples, yet hadn't realized I was alone. As I meditated on how I was feeling, I realized I honestly felt accompanied. It was no different than if there had been someone sitting in the chair across from me reading their book and sharing breakfast.

I felt surrounded by my Friend, my Father, my Husband. It was real, it was precious, it was priceless.

Sometimes when I talk to people about allowing God to be everything for them, I sense a bit of fear. They think if they give up their frustration of aloneness to God and receive Him as Friend, Father, Brother, or Spouse, it would be giving up and saying, "I will allow you to be everything to me because I'll probably not get anything anyway." It's like taking the second prize at the fair because the first one has already been taken and it's the one that's left. It's the silver, no, the bronze medal at the Olympics. I understand this feeling. After my husband had been gone for over a year, friends and family started having serious doubts that he would ever come back or that we would ever be reconciled.

Some would timidly say, and others not so timidly, "Well, you know your Maker is your husband."

I hated that verse. The theory didn't bother me. I knew God was Protector, Lover, and Spouse to all and everyone, male or female, alone or accompanied in life. But, if I accepted that Scripture as my own now in my alone life, it seemed as if I were resigning myself to the fact that God and only God was my husband. The man I had loved and lived with for twenty-five years was no longer, nor would ever be, my husband again. So I refused to accept that Scripture as mine.

"Nope, not for me, I am still praying and believing for restoration and reconciliation." If I accepted the fact that God is my husband, then why would He answer all the prayers to bring my human husband home again?"

How risky it seems to be satisfied in God. If I am satisfied and happy in God alone, won't God just stop trying to fix things for me? If I become happy in the dead-end job, why would God bother giving me another one? If I become satisfied in this two-stoplight town, why would He lead me somewhere more exciting? If I become happy with no children, why would my prayer for fertility be answered?

The whiny child gets the attention, not the contented one. When a baby wakes up crying in the night, most parents wait just a second to see if the crying stops, and if it does, then they don't bother getting up to check on the baby. Won't God do the same with us? If we keep crying, maybe He will rock us, feed us, or play with us. But if we stop, why should He concern Himself with our needs? "It's the squeaky wheel that gets the grease."

If I really and truly allow God to be everything, will I get stuck with only God?

It sounds pathetic, doesn't it? What it comes down to, we don't trust the Almighty, who spoke and it was, who fills all things, to fill the canyon in our hearts, satisfy the thirsting of our souls, or touch our tiny lives. Our need seems so great sometimes, and our God small in comparison, when it is really the other way around. He is big; we are small. God became human to become a perfect sacrifice for our needy souls, and, at the same time, to show us what He is like. God became personal. He became one of us, and we got a glimpse of who He is.

When we begin to comprehend Jesus and all He did, we can entrust our days and ways to Him and rest from our struggles to make everything work out. We can trust a God who became human, walked among us, took all our sin and shame on Himself, and rose from the dead to give life to all who ask for it. He became like us, and it helps understand Him.

A couple of years went by before I could take my wedding ring off, and when I did, my ring finger looked naked. I wanted to buy a ring I especially liked. I wanted it to be symbolic of life with God as my everything. I didn't start a frantic search, but from time to time, I looked in jewelers' windows, hoping something would catch my eye.

As I was on my way home from a conference and had several hours to spare at the Athens airport, I meandered around, killing time between flights by looking in shops and browsing through the bookstore. Then I walked into a jewelry store and saw the ring I wanted. It looked Greek; it was different, and I liked it. I knew it was overpriced, but I bought it anyway. This was an outward sign of my inward decision to allow God to fill the empty "husband" place. I felt His smile of approval and His warm presence on the last leg of my trip home as I played with the new gold ring on my finger. I knew He was gently leading me to trust Him, for everything.

A few weeks later when the credit card bill came through, I looked for the ring charge, but it wasn't on it. I thought since it had been an international purchase, it might take a while, and although I expected it to be on the next bill, it wasn't there either. There was no way for me to trace it; I didn't even remember the name of the store. After looking for the charge for a few months and never getting it, I realized that my Maker-husband had taken care of it. His gift could have been something other than a ring; it could have been anything that gives us meaning, makes us feel loved, or provides us with a feeling of completion.

Why do engaged girls show off their rings? They aren't saying, "Look at this diamond and gold band." They are saying, "Look! I am loved. I am chosen. I will be fruitful. I will have children. I will grow old with someone." The ring is only an outward sign of someone's inward decision to have and to hold, till death do us part.

How different our lives would be if we trusted Him to bring real satisfaction. We could let go of the reins of our lives, once and for all, and rest in His merciful heart and generous hand. So much frustration comes because life and circumstances don't obey our direction. If we are honest, we know there is not one single thing we can control and make go according to plan. We can't even guarantee our next breath, yet we continue to pull the strings, trying to make our life conform to the script we have written.

Nothing goes the way we visualized it, at least not for very long. The job that was going to be perfect isn't. The child that was going to be brilliant is average. The marriage that was going to be a lifelong party needs constant work. When we keep the big picture before us, we stop trying to control all the details we think will add up to a satisfying life. We must remember this is not all there is.

Jesus told a parable about a rich man who forgot this truth:

"He said, 'This is what I'll do. I will tear down my barns and build bigger ones, and there I will store my surplus grain. And I'll say to myself, "You have plenty of grain laid up for many years. Take life easy; eat, drink and be merry."'

"But God said to him, 'You fool! This very night your life will be demanded from you. Then who will get what you have prepared for yourself?'" (Luke 12:18-20)

If there is no eternity, then let's live it up and take as much as we can, experience as much as possible, and not worry about who will get hurt in the process. If this is all there is, we need to get grabby quickly, and the bumper sticker "He who dies with the most toys wins" is true.

How sad and how empty things would be if we had no assurance of more to come. Heaven is in my future, and it isn't just a comfort to me. I look forward to it with joy and expectancy.

Recently, I was in a hospital room where a twenty-nine-year-old father was holding his baby who was no longer breathing. The baby had only lived for an hour and a half; it died in his arms and was still in his arms when I arrived. We prayed. We cried.

"Have you seen how much hair he has?" his young mother asked, "See, he has my husband's nose." After the hospital staff had come for the baby, we talked of heaven. No other subject was even worth a mention. We imagined together what it must be like to grow up in a perfect place. His little lungs would be healthy there, he would breathe easy, and he had been rescued from a childhood of hardship and sickness. He would run. He would play. He would never be alone, never feel empty or sad. His future would be brilliant. Heaven is a wonderful place, filled with glory and grace, as the old gospel song goes.

I heard a sermon by Beth Moore once about our final destination. I can't quote it, but it shed light on how much the assurance of heaven changes the way we enjoy life on earth. She pointed out that the atmosphere on a trip varies according to where you are going. If you are setting out on a long-awaited family vacation, and the bags and kids are finally in the car, the climate is one of joyful anticipation. If, on the other hand, you are on your way to the school because your teenager's principal has called you or you are going to sign divorce papers, or ask the bank for yet another loan, the atmosphere in the car is dark and sad.

For all of us who know the Lord, our lives should be electric with anticipation. We are on our way to the marriage supper of the Lamb, a wedding of majestic proportions. Our Bridegroom will be waiting for us. We will be a beautiful bride compiled from every color and culture, tribe, and tongue. Everyone from the beginning of time who has ever called Jesus, Savior, will take part. It will be glorious. That is not only our destination; it is our destiny.

Paul reminds us of this truth and tells us not to get discouraged. "So we do not lose heart. Though our outer self is wasting away, our inner self is being renewed day by day. For this light momentary affliction is preparing for us an eternal weight of glory beyond all comparison, as we look not to the things that are seen but to the things that are unseen. For the things that are seen are transient, but the things that are unseen are eternal." (2 Corinthians 4:16)

When I have a rough day, I remind myself that I'm on my way to a party. When disappointment tries to take root in my heart, I look to the future. When life looks tedious, boring, or dull, I remember I am on my way to the most incredible, unimaginable jubilee. There will be music and dancing, feasting and fun, confetti and streamers, but best of all, Jesus will be there and will be celebrated in all His glory. I can't wait.

CHAPTER 15

What Comes After This

Losing two friends in a short amount of time is just not right; first Marilyn, now Jan. They were two friends whose visits I looked forward to, and I treasured my time with them. Marilyn had a laugh that could fill an auditorium. It was a beautiful, genuine laugh, which came from a person who encountered life with an acute sense of humor. I loved it. It wasn't the *snicker -snicker* about inside jokes that I might share with my sister or Mary Lou; it was a deep *hardy-har-har*. She raised the rafters and made people look over at our group with a little envy because it seemed like we were the fun bunch in the restaurant or at the airport.

When my husband left, Marilyn was a tremendous support, not so much with advice or even empathy, but with open hospitality and fun. She was always ready to drop everything to lift someone's spirit. On one visit, I mentioned to her that I had always wanted to drive to Austin to see the bats come out from under the bridge at dusk. I had heard it was a sight to behold. The words were hardly out of my mouth before she made a reservation at a B&B and we were in the car and on our way.

She was as amazed as I was when the small, gray plume started coming out from under the bridge and became a never-ending stream of bats, millions, they say. No matter what was happening around me, even if my life was falling apart, I could always watch bats come out from under a bridge. Fun and laughter bring hope to a hurting heart, and that is what she always did for mine, whether we were on trips, at conferences, or running errands.

Then she got sick, really sick. Someone recommended treatment in Germany. Since I was in Europe, I was happy and honored to drive her around. Even with the seriousness of our mission, she was able to turn the week of treatments into a pleasant time filled with good moods and humor. Sometimes, I forgot why we were even there and that it wasn't a vacation, but that my *never-smoked-a-cigarette* friend was battling lung cancer.

I miss all the things that made Marilyn, Marilyn. I miss the entire package. You lose all the details that make up the whole person, and there is so much to each one of them. There are so many things that make us, us, and when you add them all up, you have an exclusive individual to enjoy. She could keep a clean house with what appeared to be no effort and make a chocolate pie in ten minutes. Her makeup routine could have garnered her many followers on Instagram. I watched her put her face on with a quiet wonder. How did she pencil those eyebrows on so quickly and so perfectly? The clean house, the laugh, the pie, and the makeup—tied together were the one and only Marilyn whom I longed for.

The first time I flew into the Dallas-Fort Worth area after her death, I looked down from my window seat as we passed over her part of town. How odd it would be to land there now, knowing she wouldn't meet me with a smile and a hug. We wouldn't do our sidewalk-to-trunk suitcase routine, "One, two, three, LIFT!" We'd never drive out of the terminal deciding what and where to eat. Not anymore, never again.

I felt like the pilot was supposed to come on the loudspeaker and say: "Sorry, folks, we've been diverted to Houston, we can't land in Dallas anymore; it's nothing but a big hole." But we did land, and I got where I needed to be without her, and everything looked the same, but it wasn't.

And now Jan, my dear fountain of wisdom and encouragement, has also gone way too soon, too fast. As I write this, I'm trying to get tickets to Cornwall to attend her memorial. She will be laid to rest with her ancestors in a place that she loved.

We used to take long walks through the brushy woods not far from our houses on the outskirts of Madrid. I liked to tease her, reminding her to watch for snakes and pointing out fresh wild boar tracks. I got a silly pleasure out of making the stable one a little nervous, since nothing serious ever seemed to shake her. She had a corner on coaching way before anyone coined the phrase. She gave her friends the gift of undivided attention, and without any effort, she had you seeing things straighter, clearer, and with a plan for the next step. She knew how to "keep the main thing the main thing." She kept it real. Her faith was functional. Her love was practical. Her trust was solid, and the fruit from the tree of her life fell all around her.

Of course, she's been on my mind all day. I thought about her when I saw the barren window boxes and pots on my patio. She always had pansies and petunias in hers. So, I called Diana, my young friend, and asked her if she felt like going to the garden center with me. She came right over, and off we went to bring home pinks, yellows, and purples to brighten things up. We each had a spade and were busy planting. I asked her if she knew my friend Jan had died. She said she had heard, and then we started talking about sickness and death.

When Christians talk about death and dying, it always leads to conversations about heaven. Naturally. As believers, that is what we talk about because death equals heaven for us.

"What's it like?", we wondered aloud to each other.

"No sickness," she said.

"No sin," I said.

"No misunderstandings," she said.

"No strife," I said.

"No conflict! Imagine that?"

We cackled at the thought of life with absolutely no conflict. No wonder there will be no tears in heaven; we wouldn't fight with anyone. Who needed streets of gold? Just give us a gravel road with no conflict and that would be glory for us.

We talked about being able to meet someone in heaven without any complexes or insecurities. How amazing relationships will be. How precious the hope of heaven is, and how real it is to my heart.

On earth, we build and strive to make something work, to have a few things, to love a few people, and it is all a part of life here. But we need to keep our eyes on heaven, lest we despair at the frailty of life. The apostle Paul said, "If this is all there is, then we are a miserable bunch" (paraphrase, 1 Corinthians 15:19). But if anything good, sweet, or beautiful is a taste of what is coming, then we are to be envied.

Have you ever been to a party where hors d'oeuvres were passed around and you got a tiny bite of something so delicious that you thought about chasing the server down and getting the entire plate?

Any taste of goodness, joy or satisfaction in this life is a vague preview of what we will be served in eternity. Right now, things are hazy and hard to understand—often bitter or bland—*yet,* we have tasted the goodness of the Lord and even if we only had a little bite, it's enough to make us want to follow hard after Him until we see him face-to-face. That's when the fog will lift and it will all be crystal clear. It will all make sense.

Epilogue

From the time I started writing these reflections, years have gone by and things have happened; my dog has gotten old, I've married my kids off, and I just buried my mother last month. Along with the rest of the world, I'm living through a pandemic; even when time seems to stand still, the days still tick by. Someone said, "The days are long but time flies", and that's true. We often hear, "Where has the year gone?" but the most telling sign of the passing of time is when we look in the mirror and hardly recognize the person staring back at us.

The message I live by hasn't changed much. Yes, I've gotten less judgemental (bravo!) and know less now, but my days continue to be measured by the length of eternity and shaped by my longing for Heaven. I'm honored that you have read this book and hope that it has set your sights a little higher and brought back some familiar, almost forgotten, happy tune.

CPSIA information can be obtained
at www.ICGtesting.com
Printed in the USA
FSHW011951221021
85696FS